智者语录

——绝不平庸

吴 静 汤春梅◎译

青岛出版社
QINGDAO PUBLISHING HOUSE

图书在版编目（CIP）数据

智者语录．绝不平庸：英汉对照 / 吴静，汤春梅译．
—青岛：青岛出版社，2019.4
ISBN 978-7-5552-7054-6

Ⅰ．①智… Ⅱ．①吴… ②汤… Ⅲ．①英语—汉语—
对照读物②格言—汇编—世界 Ⅳ．① H319.4：H

中国版本图书馆 CIP 数据核字（2019）第 049354 号

书　　名　智者语录·绝不平庸（英汉对照）
译　　者　吴　静　汤春梅
出版发行　青岛出版社
社　　址　青岛市海尔路 182 号（266061）
本社网址　http://www.qdpub.com
邮购电话　0532-68068026
责任编辑　江伟霞　E-mail：wxjiang1206@163.com
封面设计　刘　晶
照　　排　青岛双星华信印刷有限公司
印　　刷　青岛国彩印刷有限公司
出版日期　2019 年 4 月第 1 版　2019 年 4 月第 1 次印刷
开　　本　32 开（787 mm × 1092 mm）
印　　张　8
字　　数　140 千
印　　数　1-6000
书　　号　ISBN 978-7-5552-7054-6
定　　价　32.00 元

编校印装质量、盗版监督服务电话　4006532017　0532-68068638

前 言

何谓平庸?平庸即缺乏理想和勇气,缺乏个性和锐气,缺乏创见和追求,人云亦云,模仿攀比,浑浑噩噩,碌碌无为。平庸并非平凡。两者虽然都有平常普通的意思,但平凡意味着有一颗平常心,任劳任怨地工作。平凡者有理想,可以在平凡的岗位上脚踏实地,有所进取,有所贡献,在平凡的岗位上靠着自己奋斗目标和努力做出骄人的业绩。

要远离平庸,就必须有志向。目标决定你将成为什么样的人。人生有了理想与追求,就有前进的方向和力量。如果没有理想,得过且过,到头来便一无所获。只有执着上进,不懈求索,矢志不渝,才能活出自己的精彩。如歌德所言:“人生最重要的不是处境,而是前进的方向。”要志存高远、目标远大才能让自己发挥到极致。不仅要将目标定为成功,而且要努力成为一个有价值的人。不要老是追随他人的脚步,依附如风,随波逐流。“学会按照星辰决定航向,而不是跟随每艘驶过的船只的灯光”便会避免平庸。如书中所言:“追求卓越,拒绝平庸,往往如愿以偿。”

要避免平庸，必须保持美德。世界上的杰出人物，无一不是具有美德的人物。美德提倡自制和积极的态度，提倡对世界的爱，对生命的尊重，对时间与万物的珍惜等，可以给人增添力量、勇气和自信等。一个人具有美德，才会更有活力，更能得到认可，更好地与周围的人合作，取得让人瞩目的成就。如果“认为并非是自己存在于世界之中，而是世界围绕着自己而存在”便会在工作中处处碰壁，难以有所作为。书中的许多名言都有很强的警示和激励作用。如：“只有在日常工作中尽职尽责的人，才能在重大时刻身体力行。”“美德是根，财富是果。”“自尊是一种美德，也是促使人进步的动力。”

要拒绝平庸还必须乐学好思。热爱学习是所有杰出人物的共性。就连骄傲的丘吉尔也说：“我总是随时准备好学习，即使我不总是愿意听别人的。”学习是使人持续提高自身价值的有效途径，人要有所作为必须不断学习，终生学习，“要像你会永远活着一样热爱学习”，以适应社会的发展和自身发展，“知识使人聪明，是打开智慧大门的钥匙”。书中所选名言不仅涵盖学习的重要性、学习的范围，而且还涉及对真理的追求、对社会和工作等的思考。

不平庸还必须勇于坚持。世界上所有的伟业都是坚持不懈的结果。“世间无所谓天才，天才只不过是苦干加勤奋。”“时刻牢记自己擅长什么，并坚持下去。”“在力量和耐力的比赛中，将赌注押在耐力上。”书中的这些名言都强调了坚持的重要性。在“勇于坚持”这一部分收录的内容主要强调了努力与坚持的重要性。书中最后在“把握人生”这一部分收录的名言涉及时间管理、掌控命运、对待朋友、珍惜时间等重要人生问题，强调：“人的命运主要掌握在自己的手里。”人生短暂，只有目标明确、珍惜光阴，不懈求索，才能远离平庸，让自己得到充分发展。

本书不仅为读者提供了可供思考的名言警句，而且提供了很好的翻译案例。读者可以从这些翻译体验到一些翻译乐趣。徐莉娜老师对书中的一些翻译句子做了很多修改，在此一并致谢。

译　者

目　录

追求卓越

It's a funny thing about life. If you refuse to accept anything but the best, you very often get it.

——Someset Maugham

生活很奇妙,追求卓越,拒绝平庸,往往如愿以偿。

——索默斯特·毛姆

Ten men banded together in love can do what ten thousand separately would fail in.

——Thomas Carlyle

以爱心凝聚在一起的10人团队能够完成1万个独立个体做不到的事情。

——托马斯·卡莱尔

I cannot give you the formula for success, but I can give you the formula for failure — which is: try to please everybody.

我无法告诉你如何成功,但我会告诉你如何失败——讨好每个人。

Acknowledge that you are special there's no one quite like you.

要知道你是独一无二,无人与你完全一样。

Leadership is a potent combination of strategy and character.

领导是将策略和个性有机结合起来的艺术。

You are not in charge of the universe; you are in charge of yourself.

——Bennett

你并不掌管整个宇宙，但你掌管自己。

——本涅特

There are no exceptions to the rule that everybody likes to be an exception to the rule.

——Malcolm Forbes

毫无例外，每个人都想成为例外。

——迈尔康·福布斯

It is the essence of genius to make use of the simplest ideas.

天才的实质就是利用最简单的道理。

You can travel a well-worn path through life, or go off the beaten track. If you do the latter, you may risk getting lost, but you can bet it will be an adventure.

你可以终生因循老路,也可以另辟蹊径。不走老路会迷路,冒险之趣有保证。

No great aspiration, no great genius.

没有伟大的抱负,就没有伟大的天才。

The principal mark of genius is not perfection but originality.

天才的主要标志不是完美,而是富有创造力。

Genius means the transcendent capacity of taking trouble.

天才意味着具有解决麻烦的超常能力。

Genius is one percent inspiration and ninety-nine percent perspiration.

天才是 1% 的灵感加 99% 的汗水。

The heart and soul of genius may be mad, but the mind of true genius is even as clear as the heavens seen through pine trees.

天才的心灵可能是疯狂的,但真正天才的头脑就像透过松林看到的天空一样清晰。

A genius cannot face no obstacles, for obstacles can create geniuses.

天才不可能不遭遇障碍,因为障碍会创造天才。

Genius brings the largest harm as well as the biggest profits.

天才既能带来最大好处又会带来最大危害。

A person can only show his ability when he has the right position in society to show his ability.

个人只有在社会上占据展现能力的位置,方可展现才能。

Wisdom is inexhaustible, and the further it goes, the more people need it.

智慧无穷无尽,它前进得越远,人们就越需要它。

A good horse cannot be of a bad color.

好马无劣色。

A good horse should be seldom spurred.

好马无须扬鞭。

A good tongue is a good weapon.

会说话的舌头是一件精良的武器。

No matter how tall your grandfather was, you must do your own growing.

无论爷爷多高,你必须自己成长。

The three great essentials to achieve anything worthwhile are, first, hard work; second, stick-to-itiveness; third, common sense.

——Thomas Edison

获得任何成就需要三个最基本的重要条件: 第一,苦干; 第二,毅力; 第三,常识。

——托马斯·爱迪生

There is no resting place for an enterprise in a competitive economy.

——Alfred P. Sloan

在竞争的经济中,没有企业休息的地方。

——阿尔弗雷德·P·斯隆

Anything one man can imagine, other men can make real.

——Jules Verne

但凡人能想象到的,必定有人能将其实现。

——朱尔斯·凡尔纳

He who has never failed somewhere, that man can not be great.

未摔跟头者难成大器。

The man who insists upon seeing with perfect clearness before he decides, never decides.

非要彻底明白才下决心,就永远下不了决心。

You gain strength, courage, and confidence by every experience in which you really stop to look fear in the face ... You do the thing you think you cannot do.

每经历困难,直面恐惧,便会赢得力量、勇气和信心,为不敢为之事。

You need integrity, intelligence and energy to succeed. Integrity is totally a matter of choice and it is habit-forming.

——Warren Buffett

成功需要正直、才识和精力。正直完全有赖于选择和习惯的养成。

——沃伦·巴菲特

The very essence of leadership is that you have to have a vision. It's got to be a vision you articulate clearly and forcefully on every occasion.

——Theodore Hessburgh

作为领导人的基本要求就是必须有愿景,而且要随时宣讲愿景,让人相信你所描绘的愿景。

——西奥多·赫斯伯格

High self-esteem promotes good self-confidence. Good self-confidence helps keep you motivated. You need to be motivated to brag. Self-promotion is bragging. Then again, self-promotion promotes self-confidence. Self-confidence promotes high self-esteem.

——Rochelle B. Balch

自尊强,则自信足;自信足,则动力强。要主动自我宣传。自我推销就是自我宣传。自我推销增强自信,自信增强自尊。

——罗谢尔·B·贝尔奇

Coming together is a beginning, staying together is progress, and working together is success.

——Henry Ford

一起走来是开端，一起相处是进展，一起工作是成功。

——亨利·福特

It takes a lot of thought and effort and downright determination to be agreeable.

——Ralph Waldo Emerson

要与人融洽和睦，需要认真思考，下大力气，下大决心。

——拉尔夫·瓦尔多·爱默生

Leadership is the capacity to translate vision into reality.

——W. G. Bennis

领导力是把愿景转为现实的能力。

——W·G·本尼斯

A leader takes people where they want to go. A great leader takes people where they don't necessarily want to go, but ought to be.

——Rosalynn Carter

领导带领人们走他们想走的路；一个好领导带领人们走并不一定是他们选择的但却应该走的路。

——罗莎琳·卡特

Keep your fears to yourself but share your courage with others.

——Robert Louis Stevenson

把恐惧留给自己,与别人分享勇气。

——罗伯特·路易斯·史蒂文森

Force of habit, or routine, can blind us to the wonders of the world around us.

习惯与日常事务会蒙蔽双眼,让我们对周边的人间奇迹视而不见。

The best leaders are very often the best listeners. They have an open mind. They are not interested in having their own way but in finding the best way.

——Wilrred Peterson

杰出领导者常是最善倾听者,心态开放,集思广益,不愿独断专行。

——威尔弗雷德·皮特森

When the trust level gets high enough, people transcend apparent limits, discovering new and awesome abilities for which they were previously unaware.

——David Armistead

高度信任，会消除隔阂，并发现前所未知的巨大新能量。

——大卫·阿米斯特德

Those who neither conquer others nor be conquered but get what they need are really happy and great.

——Goethe

不靠征服别人或者服从别人便能获取所需的人，才是真正幸福而伟大的人。

——歌德

Crafty advice is often got from a fool.

高见常出自愚者之口。

The fragrance of the rose lingers in the mind long after it has lost its first bloom.

玫瑰花谢，玫瑰香长留心间。

When you feel overwhelmed by life's challenges, look back at the past and remember difficult times you've survived.

面临人生严峻挑战时，回顾曾有过的逆袭经历。

Men of genius are meteors destined to be consumed in lighting up their century.

天才人物就像流星一样注定要燃烧自己,照亮所处的时代。

The first and the last a genius requires is the love of truth.

天才自始至终所需要的就是对真理的热爱。

Only the combination of genius and science can produce the largest effect.

天才只有和科学结合,才能产生最大的效果。

Hide not your talents, they for use were made. What's a sundial in the shade?

不要隐藏天赋,天赋就是为使用而生。日晷放在暗处有何用?

A genius always finds himself born one century earlier.

天才总是发现自己早生了一个世纪。

Genius is formed in quietude, character in the stream of life.

天才形成于平静之中，性格生成于生活溪流中。

Don’t go looking for opportunities — instead, make them happen.

不要寻找机会，而要创造机会。

There is a history in all men’s lives.

——William Shakespeare

所有人的生活都有一部历史。

——威廉·莎士比亚

Disappointment can only hurt you for as long as you let it; instead of looking back, try to move on, to the next challenge.

不要让失望的情绪伤害你，不要向后看，努力前行，面对下一次挑战。

However long the night, the dawn will surely break.

夜无论多漫长，黎明肯定会到来。

Almost all our faults are more pardonable than the methods we resort to to hide them.

几乎所有的错误都可以原谅,相比之下,隐瞒这些错误的方法不可原谅。

A man isn't poor if he can still laugh.

—— Raymond Hitchcock

尚能笑者不贫。

——雷蒙德·希契科克

The world breaks everyone and afterward many are strong at the broken places.

——Ernest Hemingway

世界会打击每一个人,但经历打击后,许多人在受伤的地方变得坚强。

——欧内斯特·海明威

Life with fools consists in drinking; with the wise man living's thinking.

傻瓜的生活在于饮酒取乐;智者的生活在于不断思索。

Talent without luster along itself can only shine in practice.

才能本身并没有光泽，只有在实践中才发出光彩。

A man can get discouraged many times, but he is not a failure until he begins to blame somebody else and stops trying.

除非开始抱怨别人，停止尝试，遭遇很多挫折并非意味着失败。

You know far more than you know you know. Never ask, "Can I do this?" Ask instead, "How can I do this?"

——Dan Zadra

你所知道的远超你认为你所知道的。一定不要问我能干吗，要问我该如何干。

——丹·扎德拉

Talent is not richly endowed rights by nature to few, but everyone's reliable property.

才能不是赋予少数人的特权，而是给予每个人的可靠财富。

Use the word "impossible" with the greatest caution.

凡事皆有可能。

There is no security on this earth. Only opportunity.

——Douglas MacArthur

世上没有稳操胜券的事情,只能捕捉机遇。

——道格拉斯·麦克阿瑟

If you're already walking on thin ice, you might as well dance.

——Gil Atkinson

既然已经在薄冰上行走,就不妨在上面跳舞。

——吉尔·阿特金森

Identify your strengths and weaknesses as a person. Then work on the strengths!

发现自己的优缺点,然后扬长避短。

Identify irrational and unhelpful thoughts, and learn to deal with them.

发现自己不理智、无助的思想根源,然后设法摆脱掉。

A cautious mind is the half of wisdom.

谨慎小心近于明智。

You can judge your age by the amount of pain you feel when you come in contact with a new idea.

——Pearl S. Buck

面对新观念所感到受冲击的程度是判断年龄大小的标志。

——赛珍珠

Anyone can stumble and fall, but a great person won't lie there and make it home.

谁都会摔倒,但伟人不会躺在那里心安理得。

Life will knock us down, but we can choose whether or not to get back up.

生活有时会把我们打倒,但我们可以选择是否要重新爬起来。

You do what you can for as long as you can, and when you finally can't, you do the next best thing. You back up but you don't give up.

—— Chuck Yeager

只要能做就做下去,最后做不了时,再做另外最好的事情。可以退一步,但决不放弃。

——查克 · 叶格

Real difficulties can be overcome; it is only the imaginary ones that are unconquerable.

——Theodore Vail

真正的困难可以克服,只有想象中的困难无法战胜。

——西奥多·威尔

Don't argue for other people's weaknesses. Don't argue for your own. When you make a mistake, admit it, correct it, and learn from it — immediately.

——Steven Covey

不要为别人的缺点辩护,也不要为自己的缺点辩护,犯错就马上承认,改正,吸取教训。

——斯泰文·科维

Life is but a hard and tortuous journey.

人生即是一段艰难曲折的旅程。

Real friendship is shown in times of trouble; prosperity is full of friends.

——Euripides

患难见挚友,发达多朋友。

——欧里庇得斯

If you take any activity, any art, any discipline, any skill, take it and push it as far as it will go ... push it to the wildest edge of edges, then you force it into the realm of magic.

——Tom Robbins

采取任何行动，执行任何纪律，从事任何艺术和技能，都要拼全力向前推进，将其推向极致，直到产生奇迹。

——汤姆·罗宾斯

Victory belongs to the most persevering.

——Napoleon Bonaparte

胜利属于坚韧不拔者。

——拿破仑·波拿巴

Live as though you intend to live forever, and work as though your strength were limitless.

——S. Bernhardt

活得如同生命永恒；干起来如同力量无限。

——S·波恩哈特

On life's earnest battle they only prevail, who daily march onward and never say fail.

在人生这场重要的战斗中，每日奋勇前进，决不言败者必胜。

No road of flowers lead to glory.

没有一条铺满鲜花的路通往光荣。

Good courage breaks bad luck.

勇气可以改变厄运。

Relationship is a bowl made of mud, so it's fragile; diploma is a bowl made of iron; ability is a bowl made of gold, so it's increasingly valuable.

关系是泥饭碗,会碎;文凭是铁饭碗,会锈;本事是金饭碗,会升值。

Fortune shows her power when there is no wise preparation for resisting her.

没有做好明智的准备与命运抗争,命运便显淫威。

Today's opportunity erase yesterday's failures.

——Gene Brown

今日的机遇可消除昨日的失败。

——吉恩·布朗

Go confidently in your dreams. Live the life you have imagined.

——Henry David Thoreau

大胆想象,过自己想过的日子。

——亨利·大卫·梭罗

It's hard to accept failure, but sometimes even harder to live with success.

接受失败很困难,与成功相伴更难。

There are only two ways to live your life. One is as though nothing is a miracle. The other is as if everything is.

——Albert Einstein

只有两种生活方式:好像没有什么奇迹,好像一切都是奇迹。

——阿尔伯特·爱因斯坦

Success has many fathers, while failure is an orphan.

成功有多父,失败是孤儿。

When you feel angry, upset, or at odds with yourself, ask the question: what is it I want? You may find you already have more than you realized.

如果愤怒,不安,与自己过不去,那就扪心自问想要什么呢?你会发现所得已经超出意料。

Attitude is a little thing that makes a big difference.

——Winston Churchill

态度事小,事关重大。

——温斯顿·丘吉尔

Your fate is not decided for you. You must create it, and follow it.

命运并非天注定,必须创造命运,并追随命运。

It's better to have fought and lost, than never to have fought at all.

——A. H. Clough

战败强于从未奋战。

——A·H·克拉夫

Victory is a thing of the will.

——Ferdinand Foch

胜利源于意志。

——费迪南·福煦

It's your job to accept the part without complaint and to make the most of it. Give a great performance.

毫无怨言地接受你的分内工作，并充分利用工作出色地表现自己。

Courage is not the absence of fear, but rather the judgment that something is more important than fear.

——Ambrose Redman

有勇气并非不害怕，而是想着更重要的事情顾不了恐惧。

——安布罗斯·瑞德曼

If you are faced with an adversity, turn to yourself and look for the proper resource. If it's a physical challenge, then stamina is required, if you encounter an attractive person, then self-restraint may be called for — if frustrated, patience is needed.

遇到问题，自寻良方。体力挑战，就体力应对，若遇佳人，保持克制，若遇挫折，需要耐心。

With time, you increase the habit of bringing forth the appropriate inner resources to deal with each trial, and the battles are more easily won.

随着年龄增长，增强自己设法解决问题的习惯，这样问题更容易解决。

If you focus on something that is not within your control, you will be neglecting those things that you are capable of influencing.

专注于掌控范围之外的东西，会忽视你所能施加影响的事情。

Courage doesn't always roar. Sometimes courage is the little voice at the end of the day that says I'll try again tomorrow.

——Mary Anne Radmacher

勇气并非总是咆哮。一天结束时，勇气有时会轻声说道明天我要继续尝试。

——玛丽・安妮・拉德马赫

Whatever course you decide upon, there is always someone to tell you that you are wrong. There are always difficulties arising which tempt you to believe that your critics are right. To map out a course of action and follow it to an end requires courage.

—— Ralph Waldo Emerson

无论你决定做什么，总有人说错，总有困难让你怀疑他们批评得对。按照行动路线图坚持到底需要勇气。

——拉尔夫·瓦尔多·爱默生

It takes courage to stand up and speak; it also takes courage to sit down and listen.

——Winston Churchill

站起来说话需要勇气，坐下来倾听也需要勇气。

——温斯顿·丘吉尔

Acceptance of what has happened is the first step to overcome the consequences of any misfortune.

——William James

接受现实是消除任何灾难后果的第一步。

——威廉·詹姆斯

It's time to stop making excuses and put your beliefs into action. Participate. The longer you wait, the more you become weighted down by mediocrity and insult your better nature.

不要找借口，相信自己的行动，参与解决问题。越等待越平庸，越降低品格。

A genius is a man who does unique things of which nobody would expect him to be capable.

天才是指完成没人认为他能完成独特之事的人。

The function of genius is not to give new answers, but pose new questions which time and mediocrity can resolve.

天才的职责不是给出新的答案,而是提出时代和常人能解决的新问题。

Adversity is the ladder of climbing high for the genius, and the bottomless abyss for the weak.

逆境是天才的晋身之阶,是弱者的无底深渊。

It's your attitude, not your aptitude, which determines your altitude in life.

态度而非天赋决定生活的高度。

The worst bankrupt is the person who has lost his enthusiasm.

——H. W. Amold

最惨的破产就是丧失自己的热情。

——H · W · 阿诺德

In the end, it's not the years in your life that count, it's the life in your years.

最后重要的不在于活了多少年，而在于如何活了这些年。

He who postpones the hour of living rightly is like the fool who waits for the river to run out before he crosses.

——Horace

生活中不能及时纠错，如同傻瓜等水流完过河。

——贺拉斯

If you make a mistake, don't keep going over it. Acknowledge it, try to make amends, and then forget about it.

若犯了错，不要重蹈覆辙，要亡羊补牢，不要耿耿于怀。

To conquer without risk is to triumph without glory.

—— Pierre Corneille

征服若无风险，胜者便无光环。

——皮埃尔·高乃依

That is the principal thing—not to remain with the dream, with the intention, with the being-in-the-mood, but always forcibly to convert it into all things.

——Rainer Maria Rilke

重要的是不要总梦想，总打算，总跃跃欲试，而要总奋力将其转化为成果。

——莱纳·玛利亚·里尔克

Now if you are going to win any battle you have to do one thing. You have to make the mind run the body. Never let the body tell the mind what to do. The body will always give up. It is always tired morning, noon, and night. But the body is never tired if the mind is not tired...You've always got to make the mind take over and keep going.

——George S. Patton

要赢得任何战役，必须让头脑战胜身体，不要让身体命令头脑，身体总是退缩，从早到晚都疲倦，但是头脑不疲倦身体就不会疲倦。一定要叫头脑占上风保持运转。

——乔治·S·巴顿

I never lost a game; sometimes I just ran out of time.

—— Bobby Layne

我从未输过比赛，有时只是因为时间到了。

——鲍比·莱恩

The question is not whether you're frightened or not, but whether you or your fear is in control. If you say, "I won't be frightened," and then experience fear, most likely you'll succumb to it, because you're paying attention to it. The correct thing to tell yourself is, "If I do get frightened, I will stay in command."

——Herbert Fensterheim

问题不在于你是否恐惧,而在于恐惧是否可控。如果你说不怕,然后面对恐惧,很可能怕了,因为你专注。面临恐惧时,正确的办法是告诉自己:"若恐惧要保持镇静。"

——赫伯特·费斯特汉

Change only favors minds that are diligently looking and preparing for discovery.

——Louis Pasteur

变化只青睐那些努力寻找时机并对伺机而动的人。

——路易斯·巴斯德

He who fears being conquered is sure of defeat.

——Napoleon Bonaparte

怕吃败仗的人必打败仗。

——拿破仑·波拿巴

Soul is not a bottle to be filled with but a stove to be made fire with.

灵魂不是一只要注满的瓶子,而是一个要生火的炉子。

Ability is what you're capable of doing. Motivation determines what you do. Attitude determines how well you do it.

能力就是你能做什么事,动力决定你做什么,态度决定你做得好坏。

Prepare. The time to win your battle is before it starts.

——Frederick W. Lewis

做好准备,赢得战役的时间是在战前。

——弗雷德里克·W·刘易斯

Take your job seriously but learn to laugh at yourself.

认真对待工作,但学会自嘲。

Formula for success: underpromise and overdeliver.

成功的办法就是少许诺,多兑现。

All life is a chance. The person who goes farthest is

generally the one who is willing to do and dare. The "sure thing" boat never gets far from shore.

——Dale Carnegle

生活就是冒险。行远者一般是愿做又敢做者。求稳妥者难致远。

——戴尔·卡耐基

If you would have a thing well done, you must do it yourself.

——Henry Longfellow

要将事情做好,必须亲自动手。

——亨利·朗费罗

You can either take action, or you can hang back and hope for a miracle. Miracles are great, but they are so unpredictable.

——Peter Drucker

或采取行动,或踌躇不前而希望奇迹出现。奇迹固然很好,只是难以预测。

——彼得·德鲁克

People will try to tell you that all the great opportunities have been snapped up. In reality, the world changes every second, blowing new opportunities in all directions, including yours.

——Ken Hakuta

人们会告诉你所有重要机会都被抢光了。实际上世界时刻都在变化,迸发出新机遇,这些新机遇你也有份。

——肯·哈谷达

Every day you have to test yourself. If you don't, it's a wasted day.

——Terry Butts

你必须每天考验自己,否则这一天就浪费了。

——特力·巴茨

The biggest things are often the easiest to do because there is so little competition.

——William Van Horne

最重要的事情常常容易做,因为没有什么竞争。

——威廉·范·霍恩

It's easy to have faith in yourself when you're a winner, when you're number one. What you've got to have is faith in yourself when you're not a winner.

——Vince Lombardi

名列前茅容易自信满满，没有胜出则必须充满自信。

——文斯·隆巴迪

Wherever you see a successful business, someone once made a courageous decision.

——Peter Drucker

任何成功的事业，都源于某个人所曾经做出的大胆决定。

——彼得·德鲁克

It's a good idea not to major in minor things.

——Anthony Robbins

避免陷入琐碎的事物中是上策。

——安东尼·罗宾斯

Only begin and then the mind grows heated; only begin and the task will be completed.

——Goethe

只有着手干，大脑才能动起来；只有干起来，任务才能完成。

——歌德

Adapt or perish, now as ever, is Nature's inexorable imperative.

——H. G. Wells

适者生,不适者亡,这是自然界亘古不变、不可抗拒的规律。

——H · G · 威尔斯

A man can do no more than he can.

凡事应量力而行。

The world can be changed by man's endeavor, and this endeavor can lead to something new and better. No man can sever the bonds that unite him to his society simply by averting his eyes. He must ever be receptive and sensitive to the new, and have sufficient courage and skill to novel facts and to deal with them.

——Franklin Roosevelt

人经过努力可以改变世界,这种努力可以使人类达到新的、更美好的境界。没有人仅凭逃避现实就能割断自己与社会的联系。他必须敏感,随时准备接受新鲜事物;他必须有足够的勇气、能力和技能去面对新的事实,解决新问题。

——富兰克林 · 罗斯福

A strong, positive self-image is the best possible preparation for success.

——Joyce Brothers

积极有力的个人形象可能是成功的最好准备。

——乔易斯·布鲁勒斯

Good manners will open doors that the best education cannot.

——Clarence Thomas

得体的举止会敞开最好的教育也打不开的大门。

——克拉伦斯·托马斯

Before everything else, getting ready is the secret of success.

——Henry Ford

做好准备是成功的首要秘诀。

——亨利·福特

I never consider ease and joyfulness as the purpose of life itself.

——Albert Einstein

我从来不认为安逸和欢乐就是生活本身的目的。

——阿尔伯特·爱因斯坦

志存高远

If you don't aim high you will never hit high.

志存高远才能成就伟业。

Reach beyond your grasp. Your goals should be grand enough to get the best of you.

要志存高远,目标远大才能让自己发挥到极致。

To accomplish great things, we must not only act, but also dream; not only plan, but also believe.

——France

为了成就一番事业,我们不仅要行动,还要梦想;不仅要规划,还要坚信。

——弗朗斯

When you lose faith, you lose the essence of life.

失去信仰,便失去生活的精髓。

Without ambition one starts nothing. Without work one finishes nothing. The prize will not be sent to you. You have to win it. The man who knows how will always have a job. The man who also knows why will always be his boss. As to methods there may be a million and then some, but principles are few. The man who grasps principles can successfully select his own methods. The man who tries methods, ignoring principles, is sure to have trouble.

——Ralph Waldo Emerson

没有志向就无从干起，无从干起就一事无成，何谈成就，成就需争取。知道如何为之者永远有事做，知道为何为之者永远当老板。方法也许很多，从中选一些；原则无很多，掌握原则可成功选方法，忽略原则而尝试方法必遇麻烦。

——拉夫尔·沃尔多·爱默生

Other men live to eat, while I eat to live.

——Socrates

别人为食而生存，我为生存而食。

——苏格拉底

Intelligence without ambition is a bird without wings.

没有抱负的智慧，就像没有翅膀的小鸟。

Experience is the mother of wisdom.

智慧源于经验。

If we can first find our true purpose, and then pursue it, we may find happiness.

发现真正目标,紧追不舍,幸福感油然而生。

Some folks never exaggerate—they just remember big.

——Audrey Snead

有些人从不说大话——只是心里装着大事。

——奥德丽·斯尼德

All human wisdom is summed up in two words: wait and hope.

——Alexandre Dumas Pére

人类所有的智慧可以归结为两个词——等待和希望。

——大仲马

An unambitious man is easily carried away by victory; a short-sighted man would have an exaggerated opinion of his abilities after being praised a little.

胸无大志者容易被胜利冲昏头脑;鼠目寸光者稍受表扬就不知天高地厚。

I had no ambition to make a fortune. Mere money-making has never been my goal. I had an ambition to build.

——John D. Rockefeller

发财非我志向，发财绝非目标，成就伟业才是夙愿。

——约翰·D·洛克菲勒

Written goals have a way of transforming wishes into wants; can'ts into cans; dreams into plans; and plans into reality. Don't just think it — ink it!

——Dan Zadra

记在纸上的目标会把目标变为愿望、梦想转为计划、计划变为现实、不可能成为可能。写下自己的宏愿，不要只是空想。

——丹·扎德拉

Dream lofty dreams, and as you dream, so shall you become. Your vision is the promise of what you shall one day be.

——James Allen

志存高远，追梦才能梦想成真，梦想是对自己未来的承诺。

——詹姆斯·艾伦

The greatest thing in this world is not so much where we stand, as in what direction we are moving.

——Goethe

人生最重要的不是处境,而是前进的方向。

——歌德

Keep a daily diary of your dreams, goals and accomplishments. If your life is worth living, it's worth recording.

——Marlyn Grey

把梦想、目标和成就写入日记,值得过的人生值得记录。

——马琳·格雷

Set goals, big or small. Write them down. Be specific, rather than general.

设定目标,无论大小,写在纸上,具体详细,不要大而无当。

There is nothing like a dream to create the future.

——Victor Hugo

没有什么比梦想更能创造未来。

——维克多·雨果

Nothing happens unless first a dream.

——Cart Sandburg

什么都不会发生,除非先有梦想。

——卡特·桑德伯格

Never ignore your dreams for the future — they will help to guide you on your way.

牢记梦想,梦想指引未来方向。

All of us need solitude from time to time, to reflect on where we are, who we are, and where we are going.

我们都不时需要独自思考:我们的处境、我们的身份、我们的目标。

Failing to plan is planning to fail.

没有计划就是计划失败。

There is always hope, always a new possibility, but sometimes it may be hiding.

希望与机遇时刻都在,但并非时刻都展现在我们面前。

There's no grander sight in the world than that of a person fired with a great purpose, dominated by one unwavering aim.

胸怀大志、矢志不移者让人叹为观止。

A man is not old as long as he is seeking something. Aman is not old until regrets take the place of dreams.

——J. Barrymore

有追求者不老,后悔取代梦想,人才变老。

——J·巴里摩尔

None is of freedom or of life deserving unless he daily conquers it anew.

——Erasmus

只有让生活日新月异,才配享受生活或享有自由。

——伊拉斯谟

Those who have no self confidence in success, even though in the face of opportunity, can only get failure.

那些即使遇到了机会也不敢自信能成功的人,只能得到失败。

Courage and confidence is gained from every challenge that you meet and overcome in life.

克服生活中每一次遇到的困难都会赢得勇气与信心。

Life is too short for regrets. Learn lessons from your mistakes, and go forward.

生命短暂,后悔无益,从错误中接受教训,继续前进。

Success is the ability to go from one failure to another with no loss of enthusiasm.

——Winston Churchill

成功是百折不挠、愈战愈勇的能力。

——温斯顿·丘吉尔

Every life is a boat, the dream is the boat's sail.

每个人的生命都是一只小船,梦想是小船的风帆。

The ideals which have lighted my way, and time after time have given me new courage to face life cheerfully have been kindness, beauty and truth.

——Albert Einstein

有些理想曾为我指引过道路,并不断给我新的勇气以欣然面对人生,那些理想就是——真、善、美。

——阿尔伯特·爱因斯坦

A heart will not be hurt for pursuing a dream, when you truly want something, all the universe conspires to help you complete it.

心会因为追求梦想而受伤，你真心想要某样东西时，整个世界都会协力帮你完成。

The only limit to our realization of tomorrow will be our doubts of today.

——Franklin Roosevelt

实现明天理想的唯一障碍是今天的疑虑。

——富兰克林·罗斯福

Where there is hope, pain becomes joy.

有希望在的地方，痛苦也成欢乐。

Where there is no hope, there is no struggle.

没有希望的地方，就没有奋斗。

The most obvious sign of a great man is a strong will.

伟大人物最明显的标志，就是坚强的意志。

When your will is ready, your feet are light.

——Herbert

当你的意志坚强了，你的脚步就轻快了。

——赫伯特

Once the dream has been put into action, it will become sacred.

——Ann Procter

梦想一旦被付诸行动，意志就会变得神圣。

——安·普罗克特

If you do not plant knowledge when young, it will give us no shade when we are old.

——Chesterfield

如果年轻时不积累知识，年老时将没有乘凉的树荫。

——切斯特菲尔德

When an end is lawful and obligatory, the indispensable means to it are also lawful and obligatory.

——Abraham Lincoln

如果一个目的是正当而必须做的，则达到这个目的的必要手段也是正当而必须采取的。

——亚伯拉罕·林肯

All the advantage isn't in running fast, but rather in getting an early start.

——Rabelais

优势不在于跑得快，而在于起身早。

——拉伯雷

To accomplish great things, in addition to dream, must act.

要想成就伟业，除了梦想，必须行动。

To strive, to seek, to find, and not to yield.

——Tennyson

去奋斗，去追求，去发现，但不要放弃。

——坦尼森

Hope is a good breakfast, but it is a bad supper.

——Francis Bacon

希望是顿美好的早餐，但却是顿糟糕的晚餐。

——弗朗西斯·培根

Life does not have to be perfect to be wonderful.

——Annette Funicello

精彩的人生未必完美。

——安妮特·富尼切洛

If you wait, all that happens is that you get older.

——Larry McMurtry

如果你等待，发生的只是你变老。

——拉里·麦克穆特瑞

One of the most dangerous forms of human error is forgetting what one is trying to achieve.

——Paul Nitze

人犯错误最危险的一种就是忘记自己的目标是什么。

——保罗·尼茨

A man is not old, but mellow, like good wine.

——Stephen Phillips

人不会老朽，而是越来越有味道，就像美酒。

——史蒂芬·菲利浦

Hope deserts us at no period of our existence.

——R. L. Stevenson

在我们一生中，希望从来未遗弃过我们。

——R·L·史蒂文森

My hopes are not always realized, but I always hope.

——Ovid

并非我所有的愿望都能实现，但我总是满怀希望。

——奥维德

One may miss the mark by aiming too high as too low.

——Thomas Fuller

一个目标过高和过低都会偏离靶心。

——托马斯·富勒

If a person lacks a beacon light—ideal, his life will be fuddled.

——Sukhomlinsky

如果一个人缺少一颗指路明灯——理想，就会醉生梦死。

——苏霍姆林斯基

Life is like travelling, ideal is its route without which, one has to stop. If life has no aim, energy will be exhausted.

——Victor Hugo

生活好比旅行，理想是旅行的路线，失去了路线，只好停止前进了。

——维克多·雨果

Hope is a motive force.

——Roman Roland

一种理想就是一种动力！

——罗曼·罗兰

Never let the reality get in the way of your dreams.

别让现实挡住了梦想的去路。

The ideal of man is always in direct proportion to his ability.

人的理想总是和他的能力成正比。

The happiest thing in the world is to struggle for the ideal.

世界上最快乐的事，莫过于为理想而奋斗。

True mastery of any skill takes a lifetime.

对任何技能的掌握都需要一生的刻苦操练。

Sweat is the lubricant of success.

汗水是成功的润滑剂。

If you are doing your best, you will not have to worry about failure.

如果你竭尽全力,你就不用担心失败。

Bravery never goes out of fashion.

勇敢永远不过时!

Those who turn back never reach the summit.

回头的人永远到不了最高峰!

Proper preparation solves 80 percent of life's problems.

适当的准备能解决生活中 80% 的问题。

We improve ourselves by victories over ourselves. There must be contests, and we must win.

我们通过战胜自己来提高自我。在这场竞争中,我们一定要赢!

Never underestimate your power to change yourself!

永远不要低估你改变自我的能力!

One's real value first lies in to what degree and what sense he set himself.

——Einstein

一个人的真正价值首先决定于他为自己设定的高度和意义。

——爱因斯坦

Storms make trees take deeper roots.

风暴使树木深深扎根。

Between the ideal and the reality, between the motion and the act, falls the shadow.

理想与现实之间,动机与行为之间,有一道阴影间隔。

High expectations are the key to everything.

远大理想是开启万物的钥匙。

保持美德

If we worry a lot, we get into bad mental habits. Rationalizing our fears is one way to banish them.

常忧虑会积忧成习，分析忧虑的原因，是停止忧虑的办法。

Try to be polite in all situations, however annoying you find people. You will feel better for it.

任凭对方如何讨厌，始终彬彬有礼，让你高人一筹。

Laziness is like a lock, which bolts you out of the storehouse of information.

懒惰像一把锁，锁住了信息仓库。

Kindness is more important than wisdom, and the recognition of this is the beginning of wisdom.

善良比智慧更重要，认识到这一点是智慧的开始。

Quiet words will win loud arguments.

沉默胜于雄辩。

Minds are like parachutes; they only function when they are open.

——Thomas Dewar

心灵如同降落伞，只有打开后才起作用。

——托马斯·杜瓦

Keep away from people who try to belittle your ambitions. Small people always do that, but the really great make you feel that you, too, can become great.

——Mark Twain

远离贬低你志向的人，小人总会贬低别人。真正的伟人会让你相信你也能成为他们那样的人。

——马克·吐温

Moral often can remedy the defect of wisdom, but wisdom will never remedy the defect of moral.

道德常常能填补智慧的缺陷，而智慧却永远填补不了道德的缺陷。

Live so that when your children think of fairness and integrity, they think of you.

堂堂正正做人，这样当你的孩子们考虑公正、正直时，就会想到你。

Politeness is like an air cushion: there may be nothing in it, but it eases our jolts wonderfully.

礼貌就像气垫一样：尽管里边空空，但可以很好地减少震动。

Who overcomes by forces, hath overcome but half his foe.

以武力战胜敌人，只战胜了一半。

Conceit may puff a man up, but it can never prop him up.

自负可以使一个人膨胀起来，但决不能将他立起来。

When angry, count ten before you speak; if very angry, count a hundred.

生气时，在开口说话前数到十；如果非常生气，就数到一百。

No matter how powerful you are and how great your achievements are, only by keeping your interpersonal relations with others can all this last long.

无论你多么强大，成就多么辉煌，只有保持你与他人之间的关系，这一切才会持久。

You must learn to obey before you command.

在指挥别人之前，先得学会服从。

Bona fides is the cohesive of interpersonal affinity.

真诚是人与人之间密切关系的黏合剂。

The greatest gifts you can give your children are the roots of responsibility and the wings of independence.

可以送给孩子最好的礼物,就是责任的根基和独立的翅膀。

He that always gives way to others will end in having no principles of his own.

总是对别人让步的人最后会没有自己的原则。

The key to everything is patience. You get the chicken by hatching the egg, not by smashing it.

处理一切事情的关键是耐心。要得到小鸡需孵蛋而非砸蛋。

A torn jacket is soon mended; but hard words bruise the heart of a child.

夹克破了可以马上补好,但苛刻话会伤孩子的心。

Censuring others for lacking education shows that, this person is also in short of education.

指责旁人没有教养的人，表明其本身同样缺乏教养。

Honesty is the first chapter of maxims.

诚实是格言的第一章。

Don't do anything that takes away from your self-respect.

别做有失自尊的任何事。

When we are unable to find tranquility within ourselves, it is useless to seek it elsewhere.

内心找不到宁静，别处去找也徒劳。

Anger is a wind that blows out the lamp of the mind.

愤怒是熄灭心灵之灯的风。

Anger begins from fool, ends for regret.

愤怒从愚蠢开始，以悔恨告终。

Anger is a brief madness.

愤怒是短暂的疯狂。

Anger is a thief who steals away the nice moments.

愤怒是盗走美好时光的窃贼。

An evil man obeys out of fear, but a good person out of love.

坏人服从出于怕,好人服从出于爱。

Don't pour out your heart to others until you have seen them clearly.

没有弄清对方的底细,决不能掏出你的心来。

Make it a point to do something every day that you don't want to do. This is the golden rule for acquiring the habit of doing your duty without pain.

坚持每天做不愿做的事。这是养成乐意尽职习惯的金科玉律。

If a man deceives me once, shame on him; if he deceives me twice, shame on me.

人骗我一次,他羞耻;骗我两次,我羞耻。

There are both virtue and vice in every nation, locality—indeed in everything. The wise will undoubtedly make use of the former and learn a lesson from the latter.

世间处处乃至事事皆有善恶,智者用其善而戒其恶。

One reason a dog is such a comfort when you're downcast is that he doesn't ask to know why.

狗之所以能在你情绪低落时使你感到宽慰,是因为它并不问你为什么。

Have a horse of thine own and thou mayest borrow another.

自己有马,才可向别人借马。

Forgiving and being forgiven are two names for the same thing. The important thing is that a discord has been resolved.

饶恕人和被饶恕是同一件事的两面。重要的是嫌隙得到冰释。

To receive a present handsomely and in a right spirit, even when you have none to give in return, is to give one in return.

礼貌地接受礼物,虽然你无以回报,也等于回赠了礼物。

He may freely receive courtesies that know how to requite them.

知道如何还礼的人才可随意收礼。

The jealous are troublesome to others, but a torment to themselves.

妒忌对他人是一种麻烦,对自己则是一种折磨。

You cannot prevent the birds of sorrow from flying over your head, but you can prevent them from building nests in your hair.

你不能阻止悲伤之鸟飞过你的头顶,但你能阻止它们在你的头发里筑巢。

Undertake not what you cannot perform, but be careful to keep your promise.

不要承担你不能胜任的事,而一旦许诺,就要认真履行。

A stiff apology is a second insult.

生硬的道歉是第二次无礼。

Let us never negotiate out of fear, but let us never fear to negotiate.

我们决不要因害怕而去谈判,但也决不要害怕谈判。

Don't expect anything original from an echo.

别指望能从随声附和中找到任何有创意的观点。

The better we feel about ourselves, the fewer times we have to knock somebody else down to feel tall.

自我感觉越好,就会越少贬低别人来抬高自己。

A successful social technique consists perhaps in finding unobjectionable means for individual self-assertion.

成功的社交技巧也许就在于坚持己见时能找到一种婉转的方式。

One can never consent to creep when one feels an impulse to soar.

有飞翔的冲动时,绝不会同意爬行。

It has been said that a pretty face is a passport. Virtually, it's a visa, and it runs out fast.

有人说，漂亮的脸蛋是一本护照。其实，它仅仅是一次签证，而且会很快到期。

Talents are best nurtured in solitude; but character is best formed in the stormy billows of the world.

才能在孤独中得到最好的培育，性格则在世界的惊涛骇浪中得到最好的塑造。

Everything passes— even regret.

一切都会成为过去——遗憾也不例外。

Don't accept your dog's admiration as conclusive evidence that you are wonderful.

别将狗对你的崇拜当作证据而推断你是了不起的人。

A man who uses a great many words to express his meaning is like a bad marksman who, intend of aiming a single stone at an object, takes up a handful and throws at it in hopes that he may hit.

说很多话表达自己的人就像一个蹩脚的射手，他不是用一块石头瞄准目标，而是抓起一大把石头扔过去，希望能命中。

Egotist is a man who thinks first of himself and then thinks of himself second.

自私者就是一个首先想到自己,第二还是想到自己的人。

To forgive is to set a prisoner free and discover that the prisoner was you.

宽恕如同释放囚犯,并发现释放的就是自己。

I will permit no person to narrow and degrade my soul by making me hate them.

——Booker T. Washington

无论对方如何,我不允许自己憎恨任何人来贬低自己,变得心胸狭隘。

——布克 · T · 华盛顿

Do not wish to be anything but what you are, and try to be that perfectly.

—— St. Francis de Sales

不要希望自己像其他什么,就做自己,努力完善自己。

——圣弗朗西斯 · 德赛尔斯

If you try to control the whole world, the whole world will control you.

想控制整个世界,整个世界就会控制你。

Inner peace is difficult to achieve, for it is not gained by striving, but by ceasing to strive.

内心平静来之不易,非争取便可获得,而是不争取方可获得。

But Today well lived makes every Yesterday a dream of happiness and every Tomorrow a vision of hope.

—— Kalidasa

今天幸福,每个昨天便成幸福之梦,每个明天便充满希望。

——加里陀沙

Laughter is the best medicine.

笑是最好的药。

To love and be loved is the purpose of your life.

爱与被爱,是生活的宗旨。

Only if you despise yourself can others despise you.

不轻视自己，别人也不会轻视你。

The most exhausting thing in life is being insincere.

虚情假意是生活中最累人的事情。

Plain living and high thinking.

——Willam Wordsworth

生活要朴素，思想要高尚。

——威廉·华兹华斯

No man is useless in this world who lightens the burden of someone else.

——Dickens

世上能为别人减轻负担的人都是有用的。

——狄更斯

Recognize your needs and the needs of others — that way you won't become tangled up in misunderstandings.

相互理解需求，避免产生误解。

Be a realistic optimist — have a positive outlook, but be aware of the constraints in your life.

做一个现实主义的乐观者——既保持乐观的态度，又了解生活中的局限。

Friendship is both a source of pleasure and a component of good health.

——Ralph Waldo Emerson

友谊既是快乐源泉,又是健康要素。

——拉尔夫·瓦尔多·爱默生

Throughout life, we rely on small groups of people for love, admiration, respect, moral support, and help.

——Ralph Waldo Emerson

我们整个一生都有赖于从少数人中获得友爱、赞美、尊重、道义支持和帮助。

——拉尔夫·瓦尔多·爱默生

True friendship is like sound health. The value of it is seldom known until it is lost.

——Charles Colton

真正的友谊犹如健康,只有失去时才会意识到它的价值。

——查尔斯·科尔顿

What's the use of worrying? It never was worthwhile. So, pack up your troubles in your old kit bag, and smile, smile, smile.

——George Asaf

担忧又有什么用？不值得。把烦恼塞进旧袋子里，然后微笑，微笑，再微笑。

——乔治·阿萨夫

The pain of the mind is worse than the pain of the body.

——Publius Syrus

心灵之痛远甚于身体之痛。

——普布利乌斯·赛勒斯

We are not born for ourselves.

人非为己而生。

As long as you live, you should be a man useful to the people.

活着就要做一个对人有用的人。

If we put ourselves in the place of other people, the jealousy and contempt we feel about them often disappears, and, if we imagine others in our place, our pride and conceit can be much diminished.

换位思考，对他人的嫉妒与蔑视常会消失，自己的骄傲便会大大减弱。

Make friends, not enemies, wherever and whenever you can; for if you treat others well, you'll find yourself well treated in return.

无论何时何处，交友不树敌，善待别人，必受善待。

Only a life lived for others is a life worthwhile.

——Einstein

只有为别人而活，生命才有价值。

——爱因斯坦

He is unworthy to live who lives only for himself.

只为自己活着的人不值得活在世上。

Make yourself necessary to someone.

——Ralph Waldo Emerson

使自己成为别人需要的人。

——拉尔夫 · 瓦尔多 · 爱默生

I want to bring out the secrets of nature and apply them

for the happiness of man. I don’t know any better service to offer for the short time we are in the world.

——Thomas Edison

我想揭示大自然的秘密,用它来造福人类。我认为在我们短暂的一生中,最好的贡献莫过于此。

——托马斯·爱迪生

The more things a man is ashamed of, the more respectable he is.

——George Bernard Shaw

一个人感到羞耻的事越多,他就越值得尊敬。

——乔治·萧伯纳

Travel, in the younger sort, is a part of education; in the elder, a part of experience.

——Francis Bacon

旅游对年轻人来说是一种教育,对老年人来说是一种体验。

——弗朗西斯·培根

The love of country is the first virtue in a civilized man.

——Napoleon

爱国是文明人的第一美德。

——拿破仑

Kind heart and an open mind are the best travelling companions.

善良的心灵、敞开的心扉，人生最好的陪伴。

Filter out your toxic language. Don’t run yourself down, even to be funny. When you talk in negatives, you build a negative mindset.

出言谨慎，玩笑也勿自损，消极言辞，产生消极心态。

The optimist turns problems into opportunities. The pessimist does the reverse.

乐观者转危为机，消极者转机为危。

One, though just like a handful of earth, is greatly happy if laid on the path to truth.

即使自己是一抔泥土，只要是放在通向真理的道路上，那也是莫大的幸福。

It is rare to find a selfish person who is truly happy.

自私自利者难以真正幸福。

Rudeness is the weak man's imitation of strength.

——Eric Hoffer

粗鲁无礼是弱者逞强。

——埃里克·霍夫

The test of good manners is to be able to put up pleasantly with bad ones.

——Wendell Willkie

与无礼者友好相处彰显风度。

——温德尔·威尔基

Remember to forget. Don't hold to heart what should be ignored. The best remedy for troubles is often to forget them. Train you memory and teach it manners.

记得忘记,该忽视的不要放在心上,处理麻烦的最好办法常常是忘掉,让记忆训练有素。

The greatest wealth is a poverty of desires.

——Seneca

欲望少者最富有。

——塞内加

The rate at which a person can mature is directly proportional to the embarrassment he can tolerate.

——Douglas Engelbart

一个人的成熟度与其忍受尴尬的程度成正比。

——道格拉斯·恩格尔巴特

Swiftest gratitude is the sweetest.

最快的感激最甜美。

The love of liberty is the love of others; the love of power is the love of ourselves.

爱自由就是爱别人; 爱权利是爱自己。

The end of passion is the beginning of repentance.

激情的结束就是后悔的开始。

Life cannot bloom its beautiful flowers out of lies.

生命不可能从谎言中开出美丽的鲜花。

A lie will serve your aim, but once.

谎言可以为你的目的服务,但只一次。

He that tells a lie to save his credit, wipes his mouth with his sleeve to spare his napkin.

用撒谎来保全自己的名声，就像为了节省餐巾纸而用袖子擦嘴。

Gaze not on the marks or blemishes of others, and ask not how they came.

不要盯住别人的伤疤或斑点看，不要打听它们是怎么来的。

Self-reverence, self-knowledge and self-control, these three alone lead to sovereign power.

自重、自知、自制，只有这三者是通向至高无上权力的法宝。

They who enter by the back stairs may expect to be thrown out at the windows.

从后门进去的人往往要被从窗口扔出来。

Man is his own gardener.

人是自己的园丁。

Forgiveness is a gift of high value. Yet its cost is nothing.

宽恕是价值颇高的礼物,但它的成本是零。

The soul is not where it lives, but where it loves.

灵魂不在它所居住的地方,而在它所爱的地方。

Show not yourself glad at the misfortune of another, though he were your enemy.

别人落难时不要幸灾乐祸,即使是和你为敌的人。

Don't damn the world for not returning the love you feel you've given.

不要谴责这个世界没有回报你所付出的爱。

A vain person cares his own name, the glorious one cares the cause of motherland.

虚荣的人注视着自己的名字,光荣的人注视着祖国的事业。

Vanity is arrogance's food; disdain is its drink.

虚荣是骄傲的食物,轻蔑是骄傲的饮料。

An error doesn't become a mistake until you refuse to correct it.

小错不改,就会酿成大错。

The wiser one is, the more humbly he learns from others.

人越贤明,就越谦虚地向他人学习。

We must deal with pleasure as we do with honey, only touch them with the tip of the finger, and not with the whole hand for fear of surfeit.

我们应该像吃蜂蜜那样对待享受,只用指尖蘸一点儿,而不能用整只手去抓,以免吃得太多。

Shallow streams make most din; still waters run deep.

溪浅声喧,静水流深。

Credit is an invisible power and wealth.

信用是无形的力量和财富。

There are but two ways of paying debt: increase of industry in raising income, increase of thrift in laying out.

还债的方式有两种:一是勤奋增加收入,二是节俭以紧缩开支。

It is with narrow-souled people as with narrow-necked bottles; the less they have in them the more noise they make in pouring out.

心胸狭隘的人就像小口瓶子,里面装的东西越少,倒出时噪音越大。

If he is upright, all will go well even though he doesn't give orders. But if he himself is not upright, even though he gives orders, they will not be obeyed.

其身正,不令而行;其身不正,虽令不从。

Money is a bottomless sea, in which honor, conscience, and truth may be drowned.

金钱是汪洋,能淹没廉耻、良心和真实。

The tiniest blemish can twist the roots of the heart.

最小的缺点也能扭曲心灵的根。

An honest man's word is as good as his bond.

诚实人说的话等于契约。

No one who deserves confidence ever solicits it.

——John Churton Collins

值得信赖的人从不请求别人信赖自己。

——约翰·丘顿·柯林斯

Wherever true valor is found, true modesty will there abound.

——W. S. Gilbert

凡有真勇敢,都有谦虚在。

——W·S·吉尔伯特

Frankness is the result of honesty and bravery.

坦白是诚实和勇敢的结果。

Faith is like the radar that sees through the fog, the reality of things.

真诚就像能穿透浓雾看清事物真面目的雷达。

It is not he who gains the exact point in dispute who scores most in controversy — but he who has shown the better temper.

在争论中,得分高的并不是切中要害的人,而是修养好的人。

Elegance does not consist in putting on a new dress.

高雅不在于穿新衣服。

Ingratitude is a kind of weakness; clever men are not ungrateful.

忘恩负义是软弱的表现,明智的人是不会忘恩负义的。

Man is least himself when he talks in his own person. Give him a mask, and he will tell you the truth.

当面谈话最少显露真心,戴上面具便会袒露心扉。

There is nothing noble in being superior to some other man. True nobility is being superior to your former self.

超越别人并非高尚;超越自我才是真正的高尚。

The culmination of good breeding shows more in readiness to help others than in not contending with others.

良好教养的顶点,与其说表现在不与人争,不如说表现在热心助人。

Toleration is the greatest gift of the mind; it requires the same effort of the brain that it takes to balance oneself on a bicycle.

宽容是人脑做出的最重要的决定;它需要大脑付出的努力不亚于在自行车上保持平衡。

Even staying with the closest friends, one should be polite; or impolite conducts will appear unconsciously, and so will disagreement.

即使和最亲密的朋友在一起,也要有礼貌;否则相互间就会不知不觉出现无礼的行为与矛盾。

A man has no more right to say an uncivil thing than to act one; no more right to say a rude thing to another than to knock him down.

一个人无权出言不逊,也无权行为失礼;他无权对别人说粗话,就像他无权把旁人打倒在地一样。

Be civil to all; sociable to many; familiar with few; friend to one; enemy to none.

——Benjamin Franklin

礼貌对待所有人,善于交往很多人,熟悉少数人,交上一个朋友,不树一个敌人。

——本杰明·富兰克林

The truest politeness comes from sincerity.

真正的礼貌来自真诚。

Reliance on others is necessary in life; but make sure you allow others to be reliant on you, too.

——Henry Adams

生活中信赖别人是必要的,但要确保别人也能信赖你。

——亨利·亚当斯

Politeness is not always the sign of wisdom, but the want of it always leaves room for the suspicion of folly.

有礼貌不一定是智慧的标志,但没有礼貌总让人怀疑其愚蠢。

Courtesy is built on double bases: showing respect to others and not compelling one's own opinions into others.

礼貌是建立在双重基础之上;表现出对别人的尊重;不要把自己的意见强加于人。

Courtesy is an acquired good temper which makes up for the deficiency of the nature and finally evolves into a habit similar to true virtue.

礼貌是后天获得的好脾性,弥补天性之不足,最后演变成一种近似真正美德的习惯。

Only a great character is not enough, and it has to be made good use of.

光有伟大的品质还不够,还要好好发扬光大。

A smile; a touch; a listening ear; a whispered word of comfort. Such small acts can bring a ray of light into a person's life.

微笑、轻抚、倾听、轻声安慰便会给人带来一缕阳光。

You can create love and joy in your life; your future is in your hands, and yours alone.

你可以给生活带来爱和快乐。你的未来只能由你自己掌控。

Don't spend too much time asking yourself how you feel. Rather, plan your day so you will eat well and get some exercise, both for mind and body.

不要老是想自己感觉如何,而要安排好每一天,享受美食,锻炼身心。

Character is what you are; reputation is what others think you are. Be more concerned with the first.

性格是你的为人,名声是别人对你的看法。少关心别人的看法。

Courage is the ladder on which all the other virtues mount.

勇气是其他所有美德攀登的阶梯。

A person in danger should not try to escape at one stroke. He should first calmly hold his own, then be satisfied with small gains, which will come by creative adaptations.

遇到危险,切勿马上逃离,保持镇静,机智应对,便会有所收获,有所安慰。

The true virtue is like a river. The deeper, the more soundless.

真正的美德如河流,越深越无声。

Long and steep is the path to virtue, and smooth is the way that leads to wickedness.

通向美德的路漫长陡峭,而通向邪恶的路非常平坦。

There is nothing more influential in a child's life than the moral power of an example. For children to take morality seriously they must see adults take morality seriously.

在孩子的成长过程中,榜样的道德影响力最强。要想让孩子们严肃对待道德,大人必须树立榜样。

Loyalty is the most sacred virtue in people's hearts.

忠诚是人们心目中最神圣的美德。

The most drastic and usually the most effective remedy for fear is direct action.

——William Burnham

治疗恐惧最有效的猛药是直面恐惧。

——威廉·伯罕姆

Modesty is not only an ornament, but also a guard to virtue.

谦逊增添光彩,维护美德。

True virtue is life under the direction of reason.

真正的美德是理智地生活。

Be fearful of wickedness, that's the first virtue.

害怕作恶,是首要的美德。

The high minded man does not bear grudges, for it is not the mark of a great soul to remember injuries, but to forget them.

品德高尚的人不怨恨,高尚灵魂的标志不是牢记而是忘记所受的伤害。

Charms strike the sight, but merit wins the soul.

美色悦目,美德感人。

The virtue of a man ought to be measured not by his extraordinary exertions, but by his everyday conduct.

要从一个人的日常行为而非一时的突出表现判断其美德。

There is a limit at which forbearance ceases to be a virtue.

克制有度,超限度非美德。

Real modesty is the loftiest virtue and its mother.

真正的谦虚是最崇高的美德,是美德之母。

The test of a man or a woman's breeding is how they behave in a quarrel.

判断一个人的教养,看其吵架时的表现。

Better keep yourself clean and bright; you are the window through which you must see the world.

最好使自己保持干净明亮,你看世界须透过自己这扇窗户。

Discipline is remembering what you want.

克制就是记住想要的是什么。

A man with a noble character should be a bit restrained and able to weigh the matter when in trouble, and never forget who he is.

品性高贵的人就该有所节制,遇事能权衡轻重,从不忘记自己的身份。

Character is the inner world of a person, and fame is the appearance.

品性是人的内在世界,名誉是一个人的外在表现。

A man's character is like a fence—it cannot be strengthened by whitewashing.

人的品行犹如一道篱笆——粉刷并不能使之坚固。

Temper gets you into trouble, pride keeps you there.

发脾气招惹麻烦，骄傲让麻烦不断。

People will not see you as you see yourself. If they do make assumptions about you that are not true, they simply suffer from ignorance. Being misunderstood doesn't alter the truth of who you are.

别人对你的看法与你对自己的看法不会一致，若他们的看法不对，只是不了解情况。误解不会改变你的真实情况。

Make no excuses. You don't have time, because if you use your energy that way, you won't have any energy to deal with what you need to deal with, which is overcoming obstacles and obtaining goals.

——Frances Williams

不要找借口，你没有时间，如果把精力用在找借口上，就没有精力应对该应对的事情。精力是用来克服障碍、达到目标的。

——弗朗西斯·威廉

Character is a by-product; it is produced in the great manufacture of daily duty.

性格是一种副产品,形成于履行日常职责的过程中。

A man of noble mind cannot owe his culture to a narrow circle. His country and the world must have influenced him too.

心灵高尚者的修养不会囿于狭小圈子,而一定也受到国家和世界的影响。

Flattery is more dangerous than criticism because it covers the faults that criticism will reveal.

阿谀奉承比批评危险,批评要揭露的错误却被奉承掩饰了。

Peace; love; compassion; wisdom; kindness: a way of life.

人生之道:平和,爱心,同情,明智,善良。

Money cuts us off from life, from vitality, from the alive sun and the alive earth, as nothing can. Nothing, not even the most fanatical dogmas of an iron-bound religion, can insulate us from the inrush of life and inspiration, as money can.

—— D. H. Lawrence

什么也不能像金钱一样让我们脱离生活，失去活力，远离和煦的阳光与生机勃勃的大地。甚至最严苛的宗教教义也不能像金钱一样让我们失去生命活力和灵感。

——D·H·劳伦斯

Do not meet anger with anger. Count to ten, and ask yourself, why is this person so angry? If you pay attention, you may find out.

不要以怒制怒，数十个数字，想一想这人为何怒不可遏，如果用心观察便可找到答案。

Being upright and aboveboard is a basic requirement for living and dealing with people. If one is short of this spirit, he cannot serve as a model for others even if he may excel in knowledge.

光明正大是为人处世的最基本要求，即使学识才能如何优异，如缺乏此种精神，则不足以成为别人的楷模。

To those noble-minded persons, whatever kind of job is noble.

对那些思想高尚的人来说，无论什么工作都是高尚的。

The things that are in high places are not necessarily high; those in low places are not necessarily low. This is an obvious law we have been taught by nature.

位于高处者不一定就高；处于低位者也不一定就低。这是大自然教给我们的一条明训。

Virtue is like precious odors, most fragrant when they are incensed or crushed.

美德犹如珍贵的香料，点燃或碾碎时最芬芳。

Self respect is a kind of virtue; it is also a kind of motivity, which spur one on to make progress.

自尊是一种美德，也是促使人进步的动力。

Virtue is the root; wealth is the result.

美德是根，财富是果。

Never be lewd in wealth and rank; never shake in poverty; never surrender to power.

富贵不能淫，贫贱不能移，威武不能屈。

Never look down on anybody unless you're helping him up.

除非你扶别人站起来，否则决不要俯视别人。

You will rise by lifting others.

你在举起他人时，自己也就站了起来。

Only when you have sunshine in your heart can you share them with others.

要把阳光撒到别人心里，先得自己心里有阳光。

If a jewel falls into the mire, it remains as precious as before; and though dust should ascend to heaven, its former worthlessness will not be altered.

宝石落入泥潭，仍然宝贵；尘土飞到天上，还是毫无价值。

The luster of pure gold will never fade.

纯金永远不褪色。

Judge a tree from its fruit, not from the leaves.

判断一棵树要看它的果实，而不是看它的叶子。

The reputation of a thousand years may be determined by the conduct of an hour.

千年之名也许决定于一时之为。

There are people so addicted to exaggeration that they can't tell the truth without lying.

——Josh Billings

有些人就爱夸大其词,不说谎就说不了事。

——乔斯·比林斯

Glory is all knitted from brambles.

荣誉都是用荆棘编织成的。

Fame like a river is narrowest at its source and broadest afar off.

名誉像条河,源头最狭窄,越流越宽阔。

Make us masters of ourselves that we may be the servants of others.

即使我们是别人的仆人,我们也要做自己的主人。

A true gentleman is calm and at ease; the mean man is fretful and ill at ease.

君子坦荡荡,小人长戚戚。

Example is not the main thing in influencing others—it is the only thing.

榜样不是影响他人的主要方法,而是唯一方法。

Trust is the cornerstone in a successful team.

信任是成功团队的基石。

When you meet your honorable man, remember to express your heartfelt gratitude, for he is the turning point of your life.

遇到贵人时,要记得表示发自肺腑的感激,因为他是你人生的转折点。

Only when the year grows cold can we know that the pine and the cypress are the last to fade.

岁寒而知松柏之后凋也。

An empty drum makes a loud sound; an arrogant man talks big.

鼓空声高,人狂话大。

Gratitude is the sign of noble soul.

感激是高尚灵魂的标志。

We must bury hurt with dust, but carve favor on the tombstone.

把伤害埋入尘土，将恩惠刻入碑石。

Flattery is counterfeit money which, but for vanity, would have no circulation.

恭维是假钞，没有虚荣它不可能流通。

The reputation of a man is like his shadow: It sometimes follows and sometimes precedes him; it is sometimes longer and sometimes shorter than his natural size.

一个人的名声就像他的影子一样；它有时跟在你的后面，有时跑在你的前面；它有时长，有时短。

The virtue in smooth circumstances is control; the virtue in adversity is toughness. And the latter is greater one.

顺境中的美德是节制，逆境中的美德是坚韧，而后一种更为伟大。

Moderation is the silken string running through the pearl chain of all virtues.

节制是一根绸绳，它将所有珍珠般的美德串在一起。

Modesty is to merit what shadows are to a picture, which gives it force and relief.

图画中的阴影突出主题，谦虚凸显优点。

Modesty can elevate a man's soul, but arrogance can lower it.

谦虚升华心灵，骄傲贬低心灵。

Egoists do not see the world with themselves in it, but see themselves with the world around them.

自大者看到的并非是自己存在于世界之中，而是世界围绕着他而存在。

If you think you are not conceited, it means you are very conceited indeed.

—— C. S. Lewis

自认为不骄傲自大，意味着你确实很自大。

——C·S·刘易斯

If he never sets a high value on himself, he will much surpass his self-evaluation.

如果一个人不过高估计自己，就会比自己所估计的要高得多。

If the beauty is the letter of recommendation, kindness is the credit card.

如果说美貌是推荐信,那么善良就是信用卡。

Kind hearts are the gardens; kind thoughts are the roots; kind words are the flowers; kind deeds are the fruits.

善心是花园;善思是根;善词是花;善行是果。

Beauty is indeed a soft and smooth thing, hence, natural beauty can easily slip into our soul. I must add, kindness is beauty.

美的确是一件柔滑的东西,因此自然美会很容易溜进我们的灵魂。我还要再加上一句,善就是美。

Kindness in words creates confidence. Kindness in thinking creates profoundness. Kindness in giving creates love.

言善信,心善渊,与善仁。

Wherever a noble man goes, a firm protector always accompanies him, that is, conscience.

高尚的人无论走向何处,身边总有一个坚强的捍卫者——那就是良心。

No matter what people say or do, I will maintain my kindness, just as a piece of gold or emerald.

无论世人有何言行，我都会保持善良，就像保留黄金或绿宝石。

Kindness, a common language of the world, can be felt by the blind and smelt by the deaf.

善良是一种世界通用的语言，可以使盲人感到、聋人闻到。

Don't press goodness out of your heart, and keep wickedness from sneaking into your heart with all vigilance.

不要把善良从心灵深处挤走，更得严防丑恶偷偷潜入你的心底。

The best part of the life of a philanthropist is his trivial, unknown, unmemorized philanthropic deeds.

慈善家生活当中最好的部分是不为人知、不为人记的微小善行。

The more kindness done in life, the more interests life offers itself. The two are mingled together and compensate for each other.

生活中行善越多，乐趣越多，行善与乐趣融为一体，相辅相成。

Kindness is the pride of the kind and it wakes you happy forever; it makes you endure everything and forget your troubles even in danger.

善者以善为荣，善让你快乐永存，容忍百事，居危忘忧。

The greatest pleasure I know is to do a good action by stealth, and to have it found out by accident.

最大的愉悦就是悄悄行善，然后被别人偶然发现。

Do your little bit of good where you are; it's those little bits of good put together that overwhelm the world.

所到之处行些善事，小善日积月累便会影响世界。

Do not consider any vice trivial, and so practise it; nor any virtue trivial, and so neglect it.

勿以恶小而为之，勿以善小而不为。

Conscience is nothing but other people inside you.

良心就是为别人着想。

A man's first care should avoid the reproaches of his own heart.

人首先要注意的是避免受到自己良心的谴责。

Conscience is the inner voice that warns us somebody may be watching.

良心是心灵的声音,警告我们可能有人在看着我们。

Conscience is safer than any castle made of bastion of iron.

良心比任何铜墙铁壁的城堡都安全。

A genuine conscience is a sacred temple.

真正的良心就是神圣的庙宇。

Conscience is a sentry in everyone's heart. It is on sentry to guard if we act contrary to law. .

良心是每个人心头的岗哨,监视我们别做违法之事。

One should be the first to show concern for his country and the last to enjoy himself.

先天下之忧而忧,后天下之乐而乐。

Without taking the whole game into account, you cannot really make a clever move.

没有全局在胸,下不好一盘棋。

If the brain sows not corn, it plants thistles.

思想像田野,不播种粮食,就会长满野草。

Humble as my status is, I still dare not forget to feel concerned about my country.

位卑未敢忘忧国。

It is easier to denature plutonium than it is to denature the evil spirit of man.

改变钚元素的性质,比改变人类邪恶的灵魂容易。

Carve your name on hearts and not on marbles.

将你的名字刻在人们的心上,而不要刻在大理石上。

Error is often the precursor of what is correct, but conceit is the prelude to a fall.

错误往往是正确的先导，自满是跌倒的前奏。

Nothing is easier to make people being exhausted and destroy people than being out of doing physical labor for a long time.

最易使人疲倦并受害的事莫过于长期不从事体力活动。

Regard each dawn as the beginning of your life and regard each dusk as the brief summary of your life.

把每一个黎明看作是你生命的开始，把每一个黄昏看作你生命的小结。

The ambitious climbs high and perilous stairs and never cares how to come down; the desire of rising hath swallowed up his fear of the fall.

野心勃勃的人只顾攀高枝登危楼，从不考虑以后如何下来；出人头地的强烈欲望已经吞噬了他们对摔下来的恐惧。

A man should never be ashamed to own he has been in the wrong, which is but saying, in other words, that he is wiser today than he was yesterday.

认错并不丢人，意味着今天比昨天聪明了。

We sometimes put ourselves down so as not to appear boastful to our friends. There's no need to do that. Be modest about your achievements, but proud of them also.

有时自我贬低，怕朋友觉得吹嘘。有成就，无须否认，无须吹嘘，但要引以为豪。

If you accept yourself as you are, you may find others follow suit.

接受自己的现状，别人也会接受你。

Destruction follows pride; degeneration follows arrogance.

骄傲之后是毁灭，狂妄之后是堕落。

Wealth is the test of a man's character.

财富是人品的试金石。

The best hearts are always the bravest.

心灵最高尚的人也总是最勇敢。

One never loses anything by politeness.

讲礼貌不吃亏。

Curiosity is the first virtue of the learners.

好奇心是学习者的第一美德。

Defiance of the reputation will result in defiance of the virtue.

对名声的蔑视会导致对美德的蔑视。

Like other virtues, courage is limited.

和其他美德一样,勇气也是有限的。

A woman's pure ornament is virtue, not clothes.

女人的纯正饰物是美德,不是服装。

People without virtue, often envy other people's virtues.

无德的人,常常妒忌他人的美德。

To guide sober person is a kind of virtue; to guide the drunk is an obligation to do so.

为清醒的人引路是一种美德；为醉汉引路是一种义务。

Sincerity is the best way to do things.

真诚是处世行事的最好方法。

Sincerity is the highest virtue in life.

真诚才是人生最高的美德。

Sincerity is the key to success.

真诚是成功的要诀。

If you want others to be honest, you must first be honest.

如果要别人诚信，首先要自己要诚信。

No sin is more disgraceful than hypocrisy.

没有一种罪恶比虚伪更可耻了。

An honest man is neither afraid of light nor afraid of darkness.

诚实者既不怕光明，也不怕黑暗。

Honesty is the best quality of life forever.

诚实永远是人生最美好的品格。

Honesty is the best way to move people.

真诚最能打动人心。

False sincerity is more terrible than devil.

虚伪的真诚,比魔鬼更可怕。

Honesty is the foundation of human life and the foundation of career.

诚信是做人之本,立业之基。

Those who have weak will never be honest.

意志薄弱的人,一定不会诚实。

Cheating is only temporary, and honesty is a long-term policy.

欺人只能一时,诚信才是长久之策。

Words must be faithful, and deeds must be faithful.

言行须诚信。

If a man does not keep his word, he will call someone else to break his promise.

人不守约,无异于叫旁人对他失信。

There is no richer legacy than integrity.

没有比正直更有价值的遗产。

The most immoral part of human beings is dishonesty and cowardice.

不诚实与怯懦是最不道德的。

The truth may be sad, but it is better than a lie.

实话可能令人伤心,但胜过谎言。

Sincerity and simplicity are the precious qualities of genius.

真诚与朴实是天才的宝贵品质。

When you betrayed others, you also betrayed yourself.

当你背叛别人时,你也背叛了自己。

Honesty is the wisest strategy.

坦诚是最明智的策略。

Based on honesty, happiness is incomparable.

立足诚实，幸福无比。

A bad truth is better than a good lie.

难听的实话胜过动听的谎言。

Even God helps those who are honest and brave.

甚至上帝也助诚实勇敢者一臂之力。

Honesty and diligence should be your eternal mates.

诚实和勤勉，应该成为你永久的伴侣。

Honesty is the first chapter of wisdom.

诚实是智慧之书的第一章。

The realization of virtue is due to actions, not words.

行动而非言辞成就美德。

Better lose money than lose faith.

宁可失钱，不可失信。

If morality is corrupted, interest will surely fall.

如果道德败坏了，趣味也必然会低下。

If you are true to yourself, you will not cheat others.

对自己真实,才不会对别人欺诈。

Keeping your promise is like protecting your honor.

遵守诺言就像维护荣誉一样。

Rudeness is the illegitimate child of ignorance.

无礼是无知的私生子。

Politeness is the key of human coexistence.

礼貌是人类共处的关键。

Good manners are made up of tiny sacrifice.

良好的礼貌是由微小的牺牲组成。

A smile is our language, civilization is our belief.

微笑是我们的语言,文明是我们的信念。

One's courtesy is a mirror which reflects his portrait.

礼貌展示一个人的形象。

Politeness is to the human nature as the heat to a candle.

——Arthur Schopenhauer

礼貌之于人性如同热量之于蜡烛。

——亚瑟·叔本华

Polite manners, mainly is the expression of the self-restraint.

——Edison

彬彬有礼的风度,主要是自我克制的表现。

——爱迪生

Life is short, but even so, people still have time to pay attention to etiquette.

——Emerson

生命是短促的,然而尽管如此,人们还是有时间讲究礼仪。

——爱默生

勇于坚持

All growth depends upon activity. There is no development physically or intellectually without effort, and effort means work.

活动增长才干,聪明与健康需要努力,需要工作。

Every problem contains within itself the seeds of its own solution.

—— Stanley Arnold

任何问题自身都含有化解该问题的种子。

——斯坦利·阿诺德

The greatest test of courage on the earth is to bear defeat without losing heart.

——Robert G. Ingersoll

勇气最好的试金石就是忍受失败,依然满怀信心。

——罗伯特·G·英格索尔

It is not the strongest of the species that survives, nor the most intelligent that survives. It is the one that is most adaptable to change.

活下来的并非最强者,也并非最聪明者,而是最适应变化者。

To achieve greatness, you must be prepared to dabble on the boundary of disaster.

要成就伟业，要准备好面对危机。

There will come a time when big opportunities will be presented to you, and you've got to be in a position to take advantage of them.

大机遇终有一日会降临。必须随时准备捕捉机遇。

The only way of discovering the limits of the possible is to venture a little way past them into the impossible.

——Arthur C. Clarke

发现可能性极限的唯一方法就是超越一点极限，在不可能之处探险。

——阿瑟 · C · 克拉克

Men who are resolved to find a way for themselves will always find opportunities enough; and if they do not find them, they will make them.

——Samuel Smiles

决心找出路的人总会找到足够机遇。没找到机遇，也会创造机遇。

——塞缪尔 · 斯迈尔

Our greatest glory consists not in never falling but in rising every time we fall.

——O. Goldsmith

最大的荣耀不在于从不跌倒，而在于每次跌倒之后都能爬起来。

——O·哥德斯密斯

He who loses wealth loses much; he who loses a friend loses more; but he that loses his courage, loses all.

失去财富损失很大，失去朋友损失更大，失去勇气损失一切。

One may overcome a thousand men in battle, but he who conquers himself is the greatest victor.

——Nehru

一个人能在战场上制胜千军，但只有战胜自己才是盖世无双的胜者。

——尼赫鲁

Optimist: a man who gets treed by a lion but enjoys the scenery.

——W. Winchell

乐观主义者就是被狮子逼上了树仍能欣赏风景的人。

——W·温切尔

Don't worry, it will soon pass whatever it is.

不要担心，什么事情都会很快过去的。

Suffering is the most powerful teacher of life.

苦难是人生最伟大的老师。

Don't give up and don't give in.

不要放弃，不要言败。

There are no secrets to success. It is the result of preparation, hard work, and learning from failure.

成功没有秘诀，是充分准备、艰苦工作、吸取教训的结果。

The best way to escape from a problem is to solve it.

逃避问题的最好办法，就是解决它。

With talent, you do what you like. With genius, you do what you can.

——Jean Ingress

能人做其所爱之事，天才做其所能之事。

——吉恩·英格丽丝

He knows not his own strength that hath not met adversity.

没有遇到过挫折的人，不了解自己的力量有多大。

All motivation is self-motivation. Your family, your boss or your coworkers can try to get your engine going, but until you decide what to accomplish, nothing will happen.

所有的激励都是自励。家人、老板、同事会尽力激励你，但除非你自己决定要完成什么，否则什么激励都无济于事。

Few things are impossible in themselves; and it is often for want of will, rather than of means, that man fails to succeed.

——La Rochefocauld

事情少有根本做不成的，之所以做不成，常因意志不坚定，而非办法不足。

——罗切福考尔德

Perseverance can sometimes equal genius in its results.

有时在结果上，毅力与天才异曲同工。

Winners do what losers don't want to do.

胜利者做失败者不愿意做的事。

Cowardice ... is almost always simply a lack of ability to suspend the functioning of the imagination.

——Ernest Hemingway

胆怯简言之就是几乎总无力制止想象的摆布。

——欧内斯特·海明威

While one person hesitates because he feels inferior, the other is busy making mistakes and becoming superior.

——Henry Link

一个人人感觉不行，犹豫不决，另一个人忙着犯错，强大起来。

——亨利·凌克

No one can make you feel inferior without your consent.

—— Eleanor Roosevelt

没有你自己同意，谁也无法让你不如他人。

——埃莉诺·罗斯福

We must look for the opportunity in every difficulty instead of being paralyzed at the thought of the difficulty in every opportunity.

——Walter E. Cole

要从困难中寻找机会，不要被机会中的困难吓倒。

——沃尔特·E·科尔

Take risks: if you win, you will be happy; if you lose, you will be wise.

选择冒险：冒险成功，获得幸福；冒险失败，赢得智慧。

He laughs best who laughs last.

——Waller Scott

笑到最后才笑得最好。

——沃勒·斯科特

Action speaks louder than words.

——Longfellow

行动胜于言语。

——郎费罗

Behavior is a mirror in which everyone shows his image.

——Goethe

行为是一面镜子,每人都把自己的形象显于其中。

——歌德

Deeds are fruits, words are but leaves.

——Jossph Drake

行为才是果实,言语不过是树叶。

——约瑟夫·德雷克

Something attempted, something done.

——Menander

有所尝试,才有所成。

——米南德

The success is nothing more than doing well whatever you do without a thought of fame.

——Henry Wadsworth Longfellow

成功就是好好工作不计功名。

——亨利·沃兹沃斯·朗费罗

That sort of defeats is only stepping-stones.

——Reid

挫折只不过是垫脚石。

——里德

When he is pushed, tormented, defeated, he has a chance to learn something; he has been put on his wits, on his manhood; he has gained facts; learns his ignorance; is cured of the insanity of conceit; has got moderation and real skill.

—— Ralph Waldo Emerson

身处逆境,遭受折磨与失败,可以趁机学习。逆境使变得机智勇敢,了解事实与不足,不再刚愎自用,变得稳健节制,学得一身真本事。

——拉尔夫·瓦尔多·爱默生

To be idle is a short road to death and to be diligent is a way of life; foolish people are idle, wise people are diligent.

懒惰是通往死亡的捷径,勤奋才是生活的方式。愚蠢的人懒惰,聪明的人勤奋。

Destiny is like glass; it is easiest to be broken at its most brilliant time.

命运如同玻璃,最辉煌时最易破碎。

Fortune often brings you misfortune when it brings you happiness.

命运常在给你带来幸福的同时给你带来不幸。

When someone helps you, it's your luck; when no one helps you, it's the impartial fate.

有人帮你,是你的幸运;无人帮你,是公正的命运。

Fortune is admirable, but the conquest of misfortune is more admirable.

好运令人羡慕,而战胜厄运则更令人羡慕。

The man with a new idea is a crank until the idea succeeds.

具有新想法的人在其想法被接受之前是怪人。

Don't be desperate even in great trouble. The source of life often springs out of the dark place.

在非常困境的时候也不要绝望,生命之泉往往从暗处涌出。

He that never climbed, never fell.

从不攀登的人才不会跌跤。

The worst thing in your life may contain the seeds of the best.

人生最糟的事中可能包含有最好的种子。

We cannot change anything unless we accept it.

——Carl Jung

不接受现实,就不能改变现实。

——卡尔·荣格

Labor is often the father of pleasure.

——Voltaire

劳动常常是快乐之父。

——伏尔泰

Problems loom large when men don't.

问题像弹簧,你弱它就强。

The soul would have no rainbow had the eyes no tears.

如果眼睛没有泪水,灵魂就没有彩虹。

When work is a pleasure, life is joy! When work is duty, life is slavery.

——Maxim Gorky

工作是乐趣，生活便是享受；工作是义务，生活便是苦役。

——马克西姆·高尔基

One thorn of experience is worth a whole wilderness of warning.

一次痛苦的经历抵得上无数的告诫。

The more we do, the more we can do; the more busy we are, the more leisure we have.

——William Hazlitt

越干越能干，越忙越有空。

——威廉·哈兹里特

Work is good medicine to cure sadness.

工作是驱逐忧伤的良药。

Everything that is raised to the important state has to go through spiral staircase.

任何上升到重要位置者都得经过盘旋的阶梯。

Everything is hard at the beginning.

万事开头难。

To be both a speaker of words and a doer of deeds.

既善言谈又能实践。

Bad times make a good man.

乱世出英雄。

Only they who fulfill their duties in everyday matters will fulfill them on great occasions.

只有在日常小事上尽职尽责,才能在重要时刻尽职尽责。

The shortest way to do many things is to do only one thing at a time.

各个击破是对付很多事情的捷径。

A person who is contented with what he has done will never become famous for what he will do.

故步自封者将难以再铸辉煌。

Tough-minded optimists approach problems with a can-do philosophy and emerge stronger from tragedies.

——Lucius Annaeus Seneca

坚强的乐观主义者遇事采用“能解决”的态度,逆境中表现得更坚强。

——————卢修斯·安那伊斯·塞内加

No one can degrade us except ourselves. If we are worthy, no influence can defeat us.

——B. T. Washington

除了自己,没有人能贬低我们。如果坚强,什么影响都不能击败我们。

——B·T·华盛顿

A brave man may fall, but he cannot yield.

勇者可能跌倒,但不会屈服。

The drop of rain makes a hole in the stone, not by violence, but by of falling.

——Latimer

雨滴穿石,不是靠强力,而是靠持之以恒。

——拉蒂默

Action is the antidote to despair.

——Joan Baez

行动是绝望的解药。

——琼·贝兹

In times of danger it is proper to be alarmed; but when we perceive that danger is near, we should oppose it as if we were not afraid.

危险时刻,保持警惕;危险逼近,面无惧色,从容应对。

Any activity becomes creative when the doer cares about doing it right or better.

——John Updike

做事富有创造性就是力求正确行事,精益求精。

——约翰·厄普代克

Hard work spotlights the character of people: some turn up their sleeves, some turn up their noses, and some don't turn up at all.

艰苦工作彰显人的性格:有人挽起袖子,有人不屑一顾,有人完全回避。

When truth stands in your way, it's time to change directions.

事实挡路,改变方向。

Life is not long, and too much of it should not be spent in idle deliberation how it shall be spent.

—— Samuel Johnson

生命短暂,不要老琢磨如何度过人生。

——塞缪尔 · 约翰逊

The world cares very little about what a man or woman knows; it is what a man or woman is able to do that counts.

——Booker T. Washington

知识无关紧要,本领至关重要。

——布克 · T · 华盛顿

To change one's life: a. Start immediately. b. Do it flamboyantly. c. No exceptions. Never suffer an exception to occur till the new habit is securely rooted.

——William James

要改变自己就马上行动,大张旗鼓,一干到底,绝无例外,直到新习惯根深蒂固。

——威廉 · 詹姆斯

Don't let all the things you can't do mask all the things you can.

不要让不能做的事情掩盖了能做的事情。

No pain, no gain; the choice is yours.

没有辛苦,就没有收获,决策由你自己做。

Work hard at work worth doing.

努力做好值得做的事情。

Prudence which degenerates into timidity is very seldom the path to safety.

——Viscount Cecil

谨慎过分成胆小,可并非安全之道。

——塞西尔子爵

The desire for safety stands against every great and noble enterprise.

—— Cornelius Tacitus

渴望安全就无法成就伟大而高尚的事业。

——柯奈留斯·塔西佗

Tools often deteriorate more from lack of use than over use.

工具经常是放坏了,而不是用坏了。

Price is what you pay. Value is what you get.

代价是付出,价值是回报。

The best preparation for work is not thinking about work, talking about work, or studying for work: it is work.

思考工作不是为工作做的最好准备,谈论工作或为工作而学习,是工作。

Only by benefiting widely from advice, can you take in something and understand it thoroughly, and then create a unique style.

只有集思广益,才能兼容并蓄,融会贯通,独树一帜。

Don't be afraid of death; be afraid of failing to live to the full.

不要怕死,要怕不能充分生活。

Strength is a matter of the made-up mind.

—— John Beecher

力量源于决心。

——约翰·比彻

If you plough your own furrow in life, it may yield unexpected benefits, such as enduring respect from those around you.

辛勤耕耘,会产生意想不到的好处,比如赢得周围人持久的尊重。

If you should put even a little on a little, and should do this often, soon this too would become big.

——Hesiod

不积跬步,无以至千里。

——赫西奥德

Diamond can only be found in the darkness beneath the earth. Truth can only be found in deep and meticulous thoughts.

在泥土下面黑暗的地方,才能发现金刚钻;在深邃缜密的思想中,才能发现真理。

The profoundest thought or passion sleeps as in a mine until an equal mind and heart finds and publishes it.

最深的思想或感情如同沉睡的矿藏，等待着同样深沉的头脑与心灵去发现和开发。

You will only fail if you stop trying.

若停止尝试，你只有失败。

You will be more disappointed by the things you didn't do than by the things you did. So throw off the bowlines. Sail away from the safe harbor. Catch the trade winds in your sails. Explore. Dream. Discover.

——Mark Twain

没做的事比做了的事会更让人失望，那就解开缆索，离开安全的港口，乘风远航吧。去探险，追梦，发现。

——马克·吐温

Inspirations never go in for long engagements; they demand immediate marriage to action.

——Brendan Francis

有了灵感马上行动。

——布兰登·弗朗西斯

Middleness is the very enemy of the bold.

中庸之道是勇敢之敌。

On the mountains of truth you will never climb in vain: either you will get up higher today or you will exercise your strength so as to be able to get up higher tomorrow.

——Friedrich Nietzsche

攀登真理之山,不会劳而无功:或今日有所进取,或增强力量,明日更上一层楼。

——弗里德里希·尼采

I have now spent fifty-five years in resolving; having, from the earliest time almost that I can remember, been forming plans of a better life. I have done nothing.

—— Samuel Johnson

我用55年时间下决心,从记事儿起就盘算着过上更好的日子,但我却什么也没有做。

——塞缪尔·约翰逊

It may be that the purpose of life is not to be happy, but simply to be useful; only then, if we are lucky, will happiness alight upon us, as a result of our activity.

可能生活的目标不是幸福,而只是有所作为。唯有如此,如果幸运,行动会为我们带来幸福。

Sharp tools make good work.

工欲善其事，必先利其器。

Old age, to the unenlightened, is winter; to the enlightened, it is harvest time.

老年对于无知者来说是冬天，对于受过教育的人来说是收获的季节。

Thought is ahead of action, just as lightning is ahead of thunder.

思想走在行动之前，就像闪电走在雷鸣之前一样。

Nothing but the heart can change the heart.

只有心灵可以改变心灵。

Spirit is like the seabird perching on the verge of the cliff, waiting for the moment to fly skywards.

精神如栖身于悬崖边的海鸟，在等候冲天而飞的时刻。

You cannot climb uphill by thinking downhill thoughts. If your work is gloomy and hopeless, it is because you are gloomy and hopeless. You must change your mind to change your world.

你抱着下坡的想法爬山,便无法爬上去,如果工作沉闷而无望,那是因为你自己沉闷无望。要改变世界,必先改变心态。

A man would do well to carry a pencil in his pocket and write down the thoughts of the moment. Those that come unsought for are commonly the most valuable and should be secured, because they seldom return.

最好口袋里带着一支铅笔,把自己的思想随时记录下来。那些冒出来的念头往往是最宝贵的念头,应当加以保存,因为它们一去很少复返。

The reasonable man adapts himself to the world; the unreasonable one persists in trying to adapt the world to himself. Therefore, all progress depends on the unreasonable man.

理智的人适应世界;不理智的人坚持要世界来适应他。因此,所有进步是依靠不理智的人。

If you are seeking creative ideas, go out walking. Angels whisper to a man when he goes for a walk.

如果你正在寻找创意,不妨出去走走。天使会趁人散步时在其耳边轻语。

Good work is never done in cold blood; heat is needed to forge anything. Every great achievement is the story of a flaming heart.

冷漠难以成就出色的工作,没有热度难以打造任何东西,所有丰功伟业都是激情四射的故事。

Care enough for a result, and you will almost certainly attain it.

——Williams James

关注结果,行必果几乎肯定无疑。

——威廉·詹姆斯

Life is no brief candle to me. It is a sort of splendid torch which I have got hold of for the moment, and I want to make it burn as brightly as possible before handing it on to future generations.

——George Bernard Shaw

对我来说，生命并非短短的蜡烛，而是我现在手中燃烧很旺的火把，我想在交给下一代之前让这火把尽量燃烧得很亮。

——乔治·萧伯纳

Live your life so that your children can tell their children that you not only stood for something wonderful— you acted on it.

——Dan Zadra

为崇高的事业而献身者的人生才为后人所津津乐道。

——丹·扎德拉

Don't care what others think of what you do; but care very much about what you think you do.

不要在乎别人对你所作所为的看法，要非常在乎自己对所作所为的看法。

One person can make a difference and every person should try.

——John Kennedy

每个人都能扭转乾坤，每个人都应该有所作为。

——约翰·肯尼迪

Good ideas are not adopted automatically. They must be driven into practice with courageous patience.

——Hyman Rickover

好主意不会自动被采纳,需要勇气和耐心促其实施。

——海曼·里科弗

Do what you can, with what you have, where you are.

——Theodore Roosevelt

无论身居何处,竭尽所有,竭尽所能。

——西奥多·罗斯福

There is no traffic jam on the extra mile.

往前再多走一英里便不再堵车。

To stay ahead, you must have your next idea waiting in the wings.

——Rosabeth Moss Kantfr

要处于领先位置,必须随时出招。

——罗莎贝丝·莫斯·坎特福尔

Leadership is action, not position.

——Donald H. Mcga

领导意味着行动而非位置。

——唐纳德·H·麦克贾

There is something that is much more scarce, something rarer than ability. It is the ability to recognize ability.

——Robert Half

有一种稀缺的东西，比能力还稀缺的东西，就是识才的能力。

——罗伯特·哈弗

Where all think alike, no one thinks very much.

——Walter Lippmann

思想一致的地方，谁也没有深思。

——沃尔特·李普曼

Progress results only from the fact that there are some men and women who refuse to believe that what they know to be right cannot be done.

进步只是源于坚持把难于贯彻的正确事情贯彻到底。

Anybody can come up with new ideas. What's in short supply are innovative people—persistent mavericks who believe so strongly in an idea, they will do whatever it takes to make it a working reality.

——Michael Leboeuf

谁都会有个新想法,但缺少的是标新立异、坚持不懈、坚信一个想法就不惜一切代价将其付诸实施的创新型人才。

——迈克尔·拉博夫

You can outdo you—if you really want to.

——Paul Harvey

真想超越自己,定能如愿以偿。

——保罗·哈维

You may occasionally give out—but never give up.

——Mary Crowley

你可以偶尔倦怠一下,但千万不要放弃。

——玛丽·克劳利

The winds blow strongest against those who stand tallest.

——F. C. Hayes

木秀于林,风必摧之。

——F·C·海斯

Our duty is to proceed as if limits to our ability do not exist.

我们的职责就是继续,如同我们能力无限。

Life is like a tiger. You can either lie down and let it lay its paw on your head — or you can sit on its back and ride it.

生活似虎,或被它征服,或征服它。

Argue for your limitations and, sure enough, they're yours.

——Richard Bach

强调局限性,必定受到局限。

——理查德·巴赫

Do the thing and you will have the power.

——Emerson

力量源于行动。

——爱默生

As you grow older, you'll find the only things you regret are the things you didn't do.

——Zachary Scott

随着年龄增长,你会发现只是没有及时做的事情才会让你后悔不已。

——扎卡里·司各特

Quitting your job means two things. First, you are ending a business relationship. Secondly, you are quitting, not bargaining.

辞职有两层意思:第一,结束业务关系;第二,要离职,而非讨价还价。

A good plan vigorously executed right now is far better than a perfect plan executed next week.

—— George Patton

马上即可实施的好计划远胜于下周才能实施的完美计划。

——乔治·巴顿

There are risks and costs to a program of action—but they are far less than the long-range risks and costs of comfortable inaction.

——John Kennedy

行动计划会带来风险或让你付出代价，但是安逸与怠惰会带来更长时间的风险，让你付出更大代价。

——约翰·肯尼迪

Action is eloquence.

——Shakespeare

行动胜于雄辩。

——莎士比亚

One of the greatest victories you can gain over someone is to beat him at politeness.

战胜别人的最大胜利就是礼貌地击败他。

Don't be afraid to take a big step if one is indicated. You can't cross a chasm in two small jumps.

——David Lloyd George

如果叫你跨过去，不要怕步子大，你不可能分两小步跨过一个大沟。

——戴维·劳以德·乔治

It is not because things are difficult that we do not dare; it is because we do not dare that things are difficult.

并非事情太难使我们望而却步，而是望而却步使事情变难。

A good anvil does not fear the hammer.

好砧不怕铁锤砸。

A good archer is not known by his arrows but his aim.

神箭手因其射中目标而非因其箭而闻名。

If you can dream it, you can do it.

——Walt Disney

敢想才能敢为。

——沃尔特·迪斯尼

A bad workman quarrels with his tools.

拙匠怨工具。

Between genius and diligence, I choose the latter one without hesitation. It is almost the midwife of all achievements in the world.

在天才和勤奋之间，我毫不犹豫地选择勤奋。勤奋几乎是世界上一切成就的催生婆。

Talent is the blade of the knife, and hardship is the whetstone. If the sharp blade is not used for a long time, it will rust with no use.

才华是刀刃,辛苦是磨刀石,锋利的刀刃日久不用,也会生锈,成为废物。

Only those who have the patience to do simple things perfectly ever acquire the skill to do difficult things easily.

——Friedrich Schiller

只有有耐心圆满完成简单工作的人,才能够获得技能轻而易举地完成困难的工作。

——弗里德里希·席勒

It doesn't matter how slowly you go, as long as you do not stop.

只要不停步,走多慢都没关系。

Don't try so hard, the best things come when you least expect them to.

不要急于求成,最好的事情会不期而至。

No one ever did anything worth doing unless he was prepared to go on with it long after it became something of a bore.

——Douglas V. Steere

所做之事成为烦心事之后，依然打算不离不弃，这样才能完成有价值的事情。

——道格拉斯·V·斯提尔

The height of your accomplishments will equal the depth of your convictions.

——William F. Scolavino

成就的大小取决于坚守信念的程度。

——威廉·F·斯科拉维诺

Live as if today might be your last.

把每一天当作生命最后一天来过。

Always remember what you're good at and stick with it.

时刻牢记自己擅长什么，并坚持下去。

In any contest between power and patience, bet on patience.

在力量和耐力的比赛中，将赌注押在耐力上。

Kicks only raise dust and not crops from the earth.

踢脚只会扬起灰尘，却不能从泥土中得到收获。

Do good things for others and people may accuse you of selfish motives. Do good anyway.

——Mother Teresa

为他人做好事，有可能被指责有自私的动机，但还是要做下去。

——特蕾莎修女

Try not to look at the clock too much. Remember, a watched pot never boils ...

看表没有用，心急水不开。

The most precious thing in life is its uncertainty.

—— Yoshida Kenko

生活中最宝贵的就是其不确定性。

——吉田兼好

People, like diamonds, have a basic market value, but it is only after they have been polished that the world will pay their real value.

——William Thourlby

人好比钻石,具有潜在的市场价值,只有经过打磨,世人才会为其真正价值买单。

——威廉·瑟尔比

People lack the willpower, rather than strength.

—— Victor Hugo

世人缺乏的是毅力,而非气力。

——维克多·雨果

No human can repel a firm hope.

—— Kingsley

满怀希望,所向无敌。

——金斯莱

As long as the continuous efforts, unremitting struggle, there is no things that can not be conquered.

—— Seneca

只要持续努力,不懈奋斗,就没有征服不了的东西。

——塞内加

Once you choose your way of life, be brave to stick it out and never return.

—— Zola

生活的道路一旦选定,就要勇敢地走到底,决不回头。

——左拉

We should have the perseverance, must have the self-confidence especially! We must believe, our talent is used to do something.

—— Marie Curie

我们应有恒心,尤其要有自信心!我们必须相信,我们的天赋是要用来做某种事情的。

——玛丽·居里

Perseverance is permanent enjoy.

毅力是永久的享受。

Perseverance is a measure of determination.

毅力是衡量决心的尺度。

Sooner or later, all the tenacious efforts will be paid.

所有坚韧不拔的努力迟早会取得报酬的。

A little more persistence, a little more effort, and what seemed hopeless failure may turn to glorious success. There is no failure except in no longer trying.

——Elbert Hubbard

多一点坚持,多一点努力,看似没希望好转的失败,可能转为光荣的胜利。除非不愿继续尝试,没有所谓的失败。

——阿尔伯特·哈伯德

The great things are not done by impulse, but by a series of small things brought together. And great things are not something accidental, but must certainly be willed.

—— Vincent van Gogh

伟大的事不是在冲动下完成,而是经由完成一系列的小事情;而且伟大的事不是偶然发生的,它一定要靠意志完成。

——文森特·梵高

乐学勤思

Studies perfect nature, and are perfected by experience for natural abilities are like natural plants, that need pruning by study, and studies themselves do give forth directions too much at large, except they be bounded in by experience.

——Francis Bacon

读书弥补天然之不足,经验又补读书之所缺。人的天赋犹如自然之花木,读书后方知如何修剪整枝;读书本身漫无边际,需要经验加以制约。

——弗朗西斯·培根

He dares to be a fool, and that is the first step in the direction of wisdom.

——James Gibbons Huneker

敢当傻瓜是迈向智慧的第一步。

——詹姆斯·吉本·赫尼克

Nobody teaches you how to have, and keep, a friend. It is something you must learn for yourself.

没有人会叫你如何交朋友,如何留住朋友,这是必须自己学的事情。

A lie is a lie, no matter how ancient; a truth is a truth though it was born yesterday.

谎言就是谎言,无论多么古老;真理就是真理,纵然它昨天诞生。

There are only two people who can tell you the truth about yourself — an enemy who has lost his temper and a friend who loves you dearly.

——Antisthenes

只有两种人会把你的真实情况告诉你——情绪失控的敌人和真爱你的朋友。

——安提西尼

When you hire people who are smarter than you are, you prove you are smarter than they are.

如果你雇了聪明的人,那就证明你比他们还聪明。

Wisdom lies in gathering the precious things out of each day as it goes by.

智慧源于宝贵财富的日积月累。

Other people's defects are good teachers.

别人的缺点就是自己的良师。

An invasion of armies can be resisted, but not an idea whose time has come.

军队的侵犯可以抵抗,但适应时代产生的思想却无法抵抗。

When the blind beetle crawls over the surface of a globe, he doesn't notice that the track he has covered is curved. I was lucky enough to have spotted it.

盲目的甲虫在球体上爬行时,并不知道自己走的路是弯曲的。我很幸运地发现了这一点。

Business savvy professionals know that telephone conversations remain one of the most common forms of business communication. Therefore, handling telephone conversation with class and savvy will benefit both you as a professional and your company.

精通业务的人都知道电话交往仍是最常见的业务往来形式。善于电话交谈,对身为职场人员的你和公司都大有裨益。

Many a man fails to become a thinker only because his memory is too good.

许多人没能成为思想家，只因他们记忆力太好。

To talk without careful consideration is like to shoot an arrow without a target.

没有深思熟虑的谈话，就像没有目标射出的箭一样。

A stupid person always tries to justify himself for his mistakes; but a wise man tries his best to correct his errors.

蠢材总是想方设法为自己的错误辩解，聪明人总是想方设法纠正自己的错误。

A wise man will think it over ten times after hearing it once.

聪明人听一次，会想十次。

As it is the mark of great minds to say many things in a few words, so it is the mark of little minds to use many words to say nothing.

大智者寥寥数语，即能达意；寡智者口若悬河，仍言之无物。

The easiest way for me to grow as a person is to surround myself with people smarter than I am.

对我来说最轻松的成长之路就是跟比我聪明的人在一起。

Wisdom is a tree that grows in the heart, and its fruit appears upon the tongue.

智慧是一棵树,长在心里,果在舌上。

The truth is one thing for which there are no known substitutes.

真理没有已知的替代品。

Natural abilities are like natural plants that need pruning by study.

天生的能力好像天然的植物,需要通过学习来修剪。

The candle of truth will often burn the hands of those who hold it.

真理的蜡烛常常会烧伤举蜡烛的人。

Memory is a complicated thing, a relative to truth, but not its twin.

记忆是个复杂的东西,是事实的亲戚,而非同胞兄弟。

Truth angers those whom it doesn't fully convince.

真理让不太相信它的人发怒。

Money can buy off a mean person, but it can never buy off truth.

钱可买通小人,不可买通真理。

Unthinking respect for authority is the greatest enemy of truth.

对权威盲目尊崇是真理最大的敌人。

Half the truth is often a great lie.

一半真话常常是弥天大谎。

Truth will not suffer any loss because someone doesn't admit it.

真理不会因有人否认而蒙受任何损失。

The man who finds a truth lights a torch.

找到真理的人就是点燃一支火炬。

A temporary hit depends on strength whereas a success forever is built on reason.

一时强弱在于力，永久胜利在于理。

Truth is always there. We can read its holy instructions by opening the door of our wisdom.

真理常在，需要靠心智读懂其圣意。

Truth is not a coin, which is ready there for you to put in the pocket.

真理不是现成的铸币，可以随时装入衣袋里。

We would only bow to the holy altar of truth, but not to any material authority.

我们只愿崇拜真理，不愿拜金。

To resist truth is to throw an egg against a rock.

抗拒真理是以卵击石。

Ideas are the raw material of progress.

思想是进步的原材料。

Ideas are like rabbits. You get a couple and learn how to handle them, and pretty soon you will have a dozen.

思想像兔子。你买上一对,然后学会对待它们,你马上就会有一打。

I would rather have a mind by wonder than one closed by belief.

我宁愿因好奇而有思想,也不愿因信仰而关闭心灵。

Discovery consists of seeing what everybody has seen and thinking what nobody has thought.

发现意味着看见别人见过的东西,而思考别人没思考过的问题。

Philosophy is the microscope of thought.

哲学是思想的显微镜。

Imagination is more important than knowledge. Knowledge is limited. Imagination encircles the world.

想象力比知识更重要。知识是有限的,想象力却环绕着整个世界。

To believe with certainty, we must begin with doubting.

要想确信,须先怀疑。

Truth is the child of time, not of authority.

真理是时间之子,而非权威之子。

He who doesn't understand your silence will probably not understand your words.

不懂得你的沉默的人,也不懂得你的语言。

Women like silent men. They think they're listening.

女人喜欢沉默的男人,以为他们在洗耳恭听。

Silence is the best tactics for him who distrusts himself.

拿不准的时候,沉默是上策。

Never cut what you can untie.

能用手解开的,绝不要用刀去割断。

Proper words in proper places make the true definition of style.

风度的确切定义就是在适当的场合讲适当的话。

The gate of truth is wide open to everyone.

真理之门对每个人都是敞开的。

The greatest friend of truth is time, her greatest enemy is prejudice, and her constant company is humility.

真理最好的朋友是时间,最大的敌人是偏见,永恒的伴侣是谦逊。

Truth is the property of no individual but the treasure of all men.

真理不是个人的私有财产,而是人类的共同财富。

It is not a shame for a man to learn that which he knows not, whatever his age.

——Socrates

无论年龄多大,不懂就学不为耻。

——苏格拉底

Fools learn nothing from wise men, but wise men learn much from fools.

愚者不学无术,智者不耻下问。

When the fight begins within himself, a man's worth something.

——R. Browning

一个人内心开始斗争时，他就有了价值。

——R·勃朗宁

A fool speaks without thinking; a wise man speaks every word after careful consideration.

愚人的心长在嘴上，智者的嘴长在心上。

Wit is the root of strategy.

智慧是战略之本。

Wisdom is cultivated by wisdom and conscience by conscience.

智慧要靠智慧来培育，良心要靠良心来熏陶。

A man's wisdom is his best friend, and error his worst enemy.

智慧是人的挚友，谬误是人的大敌。

The real wisdom is not being able to observe the present, but being able to predict the future.

真正的智慧不在于能明察眼前，而在于能预见未来。

You know what charm is: a way of getting the answer "yes" without having asked any clear question.

——A. Camus

魅力即不用明确地提出问题就能得到肯定答复。

——A·加谬

The foundation of true happiness is in the conscience.

——L. A. Seneca

真正的快乐基础是良心。

——L·A·塞内加

Praise is like sunlight to the human spirit, we cannot flower and grow without it.

——Graham Green

对人的精神来说，赞扬就像阳光一样，没有它我们便不能开花生长。

——格林汉姆·格林

A still tongue makes a wise head.

寡言者智。

There is no royal road to learning.

求知无坦途。

Doubt is the key to knowledge.

怀疑是知识的钥匙。

Being on sea, sail; being on land, settle.

随遇而安。

Beware of beginnings.

慎始为上。

Truth, like gold, is not less so for being newly brought out of the mine.

真理就像黄金,并不因刚从矿里开采出来而降格。

It is more valuable to seek truth than to own it.

追求真理要比占有真理更有价值。

No law has the right to obstruct the practice of truth.

任何法律都无权阻挠真理的实践。

Truth likes being refuting, for refutation makes it success. Error fears being refuting for it will fail.

真理喜欢批驳，批驳让真理取胜；谬误害怕批驳，批驳让谬误失败。

Truth is always hidden in the depth of things.

真理常常藏在事物的深处。

Bind the sack before it be full.

做事应适可而止。

Bite off more than one can chew.

贪多咽不下。

By falling we learn to go safely.

吃一堑，长一智。

By other's faults, wise men correct their own.

他山之石，可以攻玉。

A fool may give a wise man counsel.

愚人也能为智者出主意。

Growth and change are the law of all life. Yesterday's answers are inadequate for today's problems—just as the solutions of today will not fill the needs of tomorrow.

——Franklin Roosevelt

生长与变化是一切生命的法则。昨日的答案不适合今日的问题——正如今天的方法不能满足明天的需求。

——富兰克林·罗斯福

All great truths are obvious truths. But not all obvious truths are great truths.

所有伟大的真理都是明摆的事实,但不见得所有明摆的事实都是伟大的真理。

The weakness of a genius is not less than that of common people, perhaps even more.

天才的弱点并不比普通人少,也许更多。

As many languages as he has, as many friends, as many arts and trades, so many times is he a man.

——Ralph Waldo Emerson

尽可能地学会各种语言,结交很多朋友,掌握各类技艺,熟悉各个行业,如此努力方能成为一个全面的人。

——拉尔夫·瓦尔多·爱默生

Skills vary with the man. We must tread a straight path and strive by that which is born in us.

——Pindar

技能因人而异。我们必须凭借天赋执着前行。

——品达

A liar is always lavish with oaths.

骗子从不吝惜誓言。

Television can give us so much, except the time to think.

电视可以给我们好多东西,除了思考的时间。

All empty souls tend to extreme opinion.

内心空虚的人爱走极端。

If you reveal your secrets to the wind, you shouldn't blame the wind for revealing them to the trees.

如果你将自己的秘密透露给风,就不应责怪风将秘密透露给树。

Learn to say no. It will be of more use than to be able to read Latin.

要学会说不。这要比会读拉丁文更管用。

A critic is a man who knows the way but can't drive the car.

批评家是一个只认路但不会驾驶的人。

Man proposes, God disposes.
谋事在人,成事在天。

The Golden Rule is that there are no golden rules.

——George Bernard Shaw

真正的金科玉律就是世上并无金科玉律。

——乔治·萧伯纳

While intelligent people can often simplify the complex, a fool is more likely to complicate the simple.

聪明人经常能化繁为简,傻瓜可能会化简为繁。

Knowledge leads to wisdom. It is a key to open the door of wisdom, but it doesn't equal to wisdom.

知识使人聪明,是打开智慧大门的钥匙,但它不等于智慧。

A flow of words is no proof of wisdom.

口若悬河不能证明有才智。

Doubting moderately is called wise men's beacon.

适度怀疑被称为智者的灯塔。

The art of being wise is the art of knowing what to overlook.

智慧的艺术就是知道忽略什么的艺术。

Take time to read, it is the fountain of wisdom.

花时间去阅读吧,它是智慧的源泉。

In the confrontation of wisdom and fortune, wisdom, having courage and insight, can never be shaken by fortune.

智慧和命运交锋时,具有胆识的智慧绝不会屈服于命运。

There is no rose without a thorn.

没有玫瑰花是不长刺的。

You can tell whether a man is clever by his answers. You can tell whether a man is wise by his questions.

——N. Mahfouz

看一个人是否聪明要看他的答案；看一个人是否有智慧则看他的问题。

——N·马福兹

It requires wisdom to understand wisdom; the music is nothing if the audience is deaf.

——Walter Lippman

理解智慧需要智慧。音乐对于聋人什么也不是。

——沃尔特·利普曼

Not ignorance, but the ignorance of ignorance, is the death of knowledge.

不是无知，而是对无知的无知，才是真正的无知。

Wisdom is more precious than wealth.

智慧比财富更宝贵。

The wise man is always a good listener.

智者善听人言。

Knowing one does not understand is the first step to gaining knowledge.

知不足是获取知识的第一步。

Listen to what children say — sometimes they see things more clearly than adults.

孩子说话要听,有时孩子比大人看得清。

The place to improve the world is in one's own heart and head and hands.

人能改善世界的就是心灵、大脑和双手。

The best thinking has been done in solitude.

最好的思考是在孤独中进行的。

Ask yourself what the meaning and purpose of your life is. You may not discover the answer, but it will help you to focus on what matters to you.

思考生活的目的与意义,也许找不到答案,但这种思考可以让你关注重要的事。

Be curious about the world around you; try to learn as much as you can about it.

对周边世界充满好奇,学习的脚步永不停止。

The reading of all good books is like a conversation with the finest men of past centuries.

——Descartes

所有的好书读起来就如同和历史上最杰出的人谈话。

——笛卡尔

There are two ways of spreading light: to be the candle or the mirror that reflects it.

——Edith Wharton

传播光明有两种办法：当作蜡烛，或者当镜子以反射烛光。

——伊迪丝·华顿

Books, like friends, should be few and well chosen.

书籍如朋友，须慎重挑选，不宜太多。

That is a good book which is opened with expectation and closed with profit.

——L. W. Akott

开卷有所盼，闭卷有所获，可谓好书也。

——L·W·奥尔科特

Live as if you were to die tomorrow. Learn as if you were to live forever.

——Mahatma Gandhi

要像明天就会离世那样珍惜生活。要像你会永远活着一样热爱学习。

——圣雄甘地

There is no such thing as genius; it is nothing but labour and diligence.

世间无所谓天才,天才只不过是苦干加勤奋。

Common sense is usually lack of imagination, and imagination is usually lack of common sense.

常识通常缺乏想象,而想象通常缺乏常识。

Curiosity will conquer fear even more than bravery will.

——James Stephens

好奇比勇敢更能征服恐惧。

——詹姆斯·斯泰芬斯

Information is power; the information domain is the future battlefield.

——Cebrows Arthur

信息就是力量，信息领域是未来的战场。

——塞布鲁斯·阿瑟

The time to stop talking is when the other person nods his head affirmatively but says nothing.

等到对方只是点头同意而一言不发时，那就是该你停止说话的时候了。

The more intense our interests are, the more freely we can follow our hearts and be creative, so follow your heart, everything else is secondary.

越感兴趣，越能随心创造，听从内心呼唤，其余一切都是次要的。

I'm always ready to learn, even though I do not always like being taught.

——Winston Churchill

我总是随时准备好学习，即使我不总是愿意听别人的。

——温斯顿·丘吉尔

Talking is like playing on the harp: there is as much in staying the hand on the strings to stop their vibrations as in twanging them to bring out their music.

说话就像弹奏竖琴：既需要拨动琴弦奏出音乐，也需要按住琴弦不让其振动。

A little learning is a dangerous thing, but a lot of ignorance is just as bad.

——Harry Edward

知识浅薄是危险的，而无知同样危险。

——爱德华

One cannot eat one's cake and have it.

—— Davies

一个人不能把他的糕饼吃掉之后还留在手上。

——戴维斯

When we are young, we think we know everything. In old age, we find out we know nothing.

年轻人认为自己无所不知，老年人觉得自己一无所知。

Occasions are rare; and those who know how to seize upon them are rarer.

——Josh Billings

机会很少，而懂得如何抓住机会的人更少。

——乔斯·比林斯

A danger foreseen is half avoided.

预见危险几乎等于避免危险。

When you want knowledge like you want air under water then you will get it.

——Socrates

当你需要知识就像你在水下需要空气时，你准能得到它。

——苏格拉底

To spread knowledge is to spread happiness.

——Alfred Nobel

传播知识就是传播幸福。

——阿尔弗雷德·诺贝尔

Some books are to be tasted, others to be swallowed, and some few to be chewed and digested.

——Bacon

一些书可以浅尝辄止,一些书可以狼吞虎咽,而有些书则需要细嚼慢咽,好好消化。

——培根

Activity is the only road to knowledge.

——George Bernard Shaw

行动是通往知识的唯一道路。

——乔治·萧伯纳

A free man obtains knowledge from many sources besides books.

——Thomas Jefferson

一个自由的人除了从书本上获取知识外,还可以从许多别的渠道获得知识。

——托马斯·杰斐逊

Let another's shipwreck be your navigation mark.

别人的沉船就是你的航标。

Doing business without advertising is like winking at a girl in the dark. You know what you are doing, but nobody else does.

做生意不利用广告,就像在黑暗中对女孩子眉目传情。你知道自己在做什么,但别人不知道。

Snatching the eternal out of the desperately fleeting is the great magic trick of human existence.

人类生存的最大魔法,是从稍纵即逝的事物中攫取永恒。

The world is a ladder for some to go up and some down.

世事如梯,有人上,有人下。

Few rich men own their property. The property owns them.

没有多少富人拥有他们的财产;是财产拥有他们。

We need to learn to set our course by the stars, not by the lights of every passing ship.

我们应该学会按照星辰决定航向,而不是跟随每艘驶过的船只的灯光。

There's only a step from the sublime to the ridiculous, but there's no road leading back from the ridiculous to the sublime.

从崇高到荒谬只有一步之差,但从荒谬回到崇高却没有路。

You can't be afraid of stepping on toes if you want to go dancing.

你想去跳舞就不能害怕踩着别人的脚。

Compromise is simply changing the question to fit the answer.

妥协只不过是修改问题以迁就答案。

Put all your eggs in one basket—and watch that basket.

把所有的鸡蛋放在一个篮子里,然后看好那只篮子。

At times, although one is perfectly right, one's legs tremble; at other times, although one is completely in the wrong, birds sing in one's soul.

有时我们虽然理直气壮,双腿却不免颤抖;有时我们虽然完全错了,却内心欢畅。

Trouble, like the hill ahead, straightens out when you advance upon it.

麻烦,就像前面的小山,你踏上去的时候,就会转为通途。

Imagination is not to be divorced from the facts.

——A. N. Whitehead

想象不应脱离现实。

——A·N·怀特海德

We soon believe what we desire.

—— Chaucer

欲望中的东西,我们很快就信以为真。

——乔叟

A bird in the hand is worth two in the bush.

—— Heywood

手中的一只鸟胜于林中的两只鸟。

——希伍德

One swallow does not make a summer.

—— Taverner

一燕不成夏。

——泰维纳

Shallow people believe in luck, believe in circumstances. Strong people believe in cause and effect.

浅薄的人相信运气,相信条件;坚强的人相信因果。

If you can't make a mistake, you can't make anything.

一生不犯错误,就会一事无成。

A leopard cherishes his paws; a wise man his tongue.

猎豹爱惜爪子,智者爱惜舌头。

The more real interviews you go on, the more comfortable you will begin to feel, and the more likely your interview will go well enough to get an offer.

参加面试的机会越多,你就越坦然自如,面试效果亦越好,得到工作机会的可能性就越大。

A relaxed job candidate is a confident job candidate.

——Caroline Levchuck

求职时放松是有信心的表现。

——卡罗林·利弗丘科

See yourself enjoying the interaction with your interviewers, answering every question effectively and eloquently. Imagine receiving an offer and then your first paycheck. This will not only motivate you, but will also relax you.

想象一下你喜欢跟考官对话,流利而又巧妙地回答每一个问题。想象一下你得到了一份工作,而后又得到了第一张薪水支票。这不仅会给你动力,而且还会让你放松地面对考官。

Lack of preparation can lead to having an unprofessional image. And if a potential employer can't reach you the first try, you may have lost your opportunity.

——Joan Runnheim

缺乏准备,给人以不专业的形象。如果一个准雇主第一次想见你而没找到你,你也许会失去机会。

——乔恩·朗海姆

We cannot direct the wind but we can adjust the sails.

无法改变风向,可以调整风帆。

A ship does not sail with yesterday's wind.

——L'Amour Louis

昨日的风无助于今日行舟。

——拉莫·路易斯

The first step toward change is awareness. The second step is acceptance.

——Branden Nathaniel

走近变化的第一步是意识到变化,第二步是接受变化。

——勃兰登·纳撒尼尔

Today's business environment is so competitive that most resume receive only a 15-second glance.

今天的市场充满了竞争,大多数的简历只能得到 15 秒钟的过目机会。

The resume is a selling tool that outlines your skills and experiences so an employer can see, at a glance, how you can contribute to the employer's workplace.

简历是概要介绍你的技能和经历的营销工具,雇主通过简历一眼就能看出你能为公司做些什么。

Live your imagination, not your history.

——Stephen Covey

要生活在想象中,不要生活在过去。

——史蒂芬·柯维

A good example is the best sermon.

身教胜似言教。

A resume or profile is an accepted form of self-promotion and bragging, although people don't view it as a self-promotion tool. But it is.

——Rochelle B. Balch

简历或简介是一种已为人们所接受的自我推销和自我宣传的形式,尽管人们没有把它视为自我推销,但它的确就是。

——罗谢尔·B·贝尔奇

Whether or not you seek to be, you are communicating all day long, especially when you're at work. By becoming more aware of this dynamic process and the verbal and nonverbal clues that you send to bosses, coworkers, and the office staff, you can better position yourself to relay the type of message you choose.

——Jeff Davidson

无论是否故意,你整天都在传递信息,尤其是工作时。意识到这个动态过程,意识到你的话语和肢体语言在向老板、同事和其他工作人员传递信息,你就会更加注意摆正自己的位置,有选择地传递信息。

——杰弗·戴维森

Effective speaking has increasingly become a highly demanded attribute of rising career professionals. There's no getting around it—nearly every organization wants technologically competent professionals who can reasonably articulate their thoughts.

——Jeff Davidson

说话讲究效率已逐渐成为职场晋升的必要条件。毋庸置疑——几乎每个公司都想聘用既善于表达而又在技术方面称职的职场人员。

——杰弗·戴维森

Most people pay more attention to their resume instead of their cover letter; however, the cover letter is the first impression, and we all know that you never get a second chance at a first impression. If you do not grab the employers' attention and appeal to their interests right away, they will not give your resume the time of day and will immediately toss it in the trash.

——Kathlene Watson

多数求职者不重视求职信,而更注重简历。求职信是第一印象,我们都知道第一印象不佳,就不会有第二次机会。不抓住雇主的注意力,吸引其兴趣,他们就不会在你的简历上花时间,而是立刻将其扔进垃圾箱。

——凯瑟琳·华生

I forget what I was taught; I only remember what I have learned.

——Patrick White

我忘了别人教我的东西,只记得我学的东西。

——帕特里克·怀特

Learning is the enterprise of a lifetime.

——Wilson

学习是终生的事业。

——威尔逊

Live to learn, not learn to live.

——Francis Bacon

活着就要学习，学习不是为了活着。

——弗朗西斯·培根

The three foundations of learning: seeing much, suffering much, and studying much.

——Willa Catherall

学习的三个基本方法：多观察、多磨砺、多研究。

——维拉·卡瑟罗尔

When something can be read without effort, great effort has gone into its writing.

某些东西读起来毫不费力，那一定是写时相当费劲。

A leader knows what's best to do; a manager knows merely how best to do it.

一个领导人知道做好什么，一个经理仅仅知道怎样做最好。

Wisdom is to the soul what health is to the body.

智慧之于灵魂就像健康之于身体。

Wisdom is in the head and not in the beard.

智慧在于有脑子,而不在于有胡子。

From the errors of others, the wise corrects his own.

智者从别人的错误中纠正自己的错误。

Better a wise enemy is than an ignorant friend.

与其交无知的朋友,不如有聪明的敌人。

Wisdom is the gem of condensed knowledge.

智慧是知识凝结成的宝石。

He who loves truth loves it in safety and more so in danger.

热爱真理的人没有危险时爱真理,危险时更爱真理。

Everyone hopes that truth is on his side, but not all of them are sincerely ready to stand on the side of truth.

每个人都希望真理在自己一边,但并不是每个人都真诚地愿意站在真理一边。

When you feel heart contented, and ask for no more, you have found truth.

心里满足无所求，真理来到你面前。

Man approaches the unattainable truth through a succession of errors.

人类通过不断犯错误而接近不可企及的真理。

Man keeps making blunders in the pursuit of truth.

人在追求真理时是会不断犯错误的。

Adhere to truth — never shake in any circumstances.

要坚持真理——在任何情况下都不要动摇。

Intelligence will not stop at the truth already known but will advance continuously to the truth still unknown.

智者绝不会止步于已知真理，而会继续向未知世界进发。

The broadest in the world is sea, the sky is broader than sea, man's mind broader than the sky.

世界上最浩瀚的是海洋，比海洋更浩瀚的是天空，比天空浩瀚的是人的心灵。

Justifying a fault doubles it.

为错误找借口是加倍的错误。

Other people's interruptions of your work are relatively insignificant compared with the countless times you interrupt yourself.

别人对你工作的干扰与你自己无数次地打断自己相比微不足道。

Two heads are better than one.

三个臭皮匠,顶个诸葛亮。

God helps those who help themselves.

天助自助者。

Growth in wisdom may be exactly measured by decrease in bitterness.

智慧的增长可用痛苦的减少来精确衡量。

Rome wasn't built in one day.

冰冻三尺,非一日之寒。

Repetition is the mother of study.

——Di Cigen

重复是学习之母。

——狄慈根

When you still cannot say to yourself what you have learned today, do not go to bed.

还不能对自己说今天学到了什么,就不要去睡觉。

A man dies still if he has done nothing, as one who has done much.

无所事事亦难逃一死,何不奋斗终生。

All books are divisible into two classes: the books of the hour, and the books of all time.

一切书籍都可以分为两类:即:一时之书与永久之书。

Books are to mankind what memory is to the individual.

书之于人类,犹如记忆之于个人。

Books are treasure banks storing wisdom passed down from generation to generation.

书籍是贮存人类代代相传的智慧的宝库。

Friends are not books, yet books are friends Friends may betray you, while books are always loyal.

朋友不是书,书却是朋友。朋友可能背叛你,书却永远忠实。

A man becomes learned by asking questions.

善问才能有学问。

Man cannot spin and reel at the same time.

一心不能二用。

By reading we enrich the mind, by conversation we polish it.

读书使人充实,交谈使人完善。

Complacency is the enemy of study.

学习的敌人是自己的满足。

A handful of common sense is worth bushel of learning.

一些常识胜过很多学问。

Learning is an ornament in prosperity, a refuge in adversity, and a provision in old age.

学问在得意时是装饰品，失意时是庇护所，年老时是必需品。

A good book is a best friend who never turns his back upon us.

好书如挚友，永远不相负。

People die, but books never. No man and no force can abolish memory.

——Franklin Roosevelt

人会死亡，书却无朽。没有任何人、任何力量可以废除记忆。

——富兰克林·罗斯福

Reading is to the mind what exercise it to the body.

——Richard Steele

读书之于心灵，犹如运动之于身体。

——理查德·斯蒂尔

The more a man learns, the more he knows his ignorance.

学然后知不足。

Reading without reflecting is like eating without digesting.

读书不加思考,如同吃东西不经消化。

Genius only means hard-working all one's life.

天才只意味着终生努力。

Diligence and loose must keep balance, thus the balance of life will not skewed.

勤奋与放松必须保持平衡,生活的天平才不会歪斜。

Science is for those who are studious; poetry is for the sake of those knowledgeable people.

科学是为了那些勤奋好学的人,诗歌是为了那些知识渊博的人。

Diligence is the twin of wisdom; lazy is the brother of stupid.

勤奋是智慧的双胞胎,懒惰是愚蠢的亲兄弟。

Diligence is the master of time; laziness is the slave of time.

勤奋是时间的主人,怠惰是时间的奴隶。

Where there is diligence, there is success.

哪儿有勤奋，哪儿就有成功。

Diligence is the a golden key to knowledge.

勤奋是开启知识大门的一把金钥匙。

We must like bees, to pick lots of flowers, then to brew a honey.

我们须如蜜蜂一样，采过许多花，而后酿出蜜来。

Diligence is the foundation of happiness; lazy is the origin of evil.

勤奋是幸福的基础，懒惰是罪恶的起源。

Confidence comes from strength, strength comes from diligence.

信心来自实力，实力来自勤奋。

Diligence can make up for the lack of wise, but the wise cannot make up for the defects of laziness.

勤奋可以弥补智慧之不足，但智慧无法弥补懒惰的缺陷。

Diligence will bring fruitful results.

勤奋会给人带来丰硕的成果。

Wisdom comes from diligence, and great from the ordinary.

智慧源于勤奋,伟大出自平凡。

Be diligent, and stick to it! Believe in yourself, anything is possible.

勤奋,坚持到底! 相信自己,一切皆有可能。

If you do not have talent, diligence can make up for the lack of it.

假如你没有天赋,勤奋可以弥补。

You see my talent, but didn’t see my diligence.

你们都看到了我的天分,但没有看到我的勤奋。

Diligence is a kind of quality, a kind of spirit, but also the soul of a nation.

勤奋,是一种品质、一种精神,更是一个民族的灵魂。

To study hard and work hard will make the youth more glorious.

努力学习,勤奋工作,让青春更加光彩。

A man with perseverance can squeeze the water out of the rock.

有毅力的人,能从石头里挤出水。

Wisdom is out of diligence, and genius lies in accumulation.

聪明出于勤奋,天才在于积累。

The establishment of great life is not to be able to know, but to be able to do it.

人生伟业的建立,不在能知,乃在能行。

Run forward, against the cold and ridicule.

向前跑,迎着冷眼和嘲笑。

You are not afraid of difficulties, and difficulties are afraid of you.

你不怕困难,困难就怕你。

If you are strong enough, you are unprecedented.

如果你足够坚强,你就是史无前例的。

Things that are helpful to you are not all readily available.

对你有帮助的东西,并不都是唾手可得的。

People who dare to struggle are not afraid of difficulties in their hearts.

敢于奋斗的人,心中不怕困难。

Behind each of the strenuous efforts, there must be double reward.

每一发奋努力的背后,必有加倍的赏赐。

No one can give you strength except yourself.

除了自己,任何人都无法给你力量。

Every kind of trauma is a kind of maturity.

每一种创伤,都是一种成熟。

Only in sufferings can you know yourself.

只有在苦难中,才能认识自我。

It is better to be laughed at for a short while than to be laughed at for a lifetime.

宁可被人笑一时,不可被人笑一辈子。

If you want to change your destiny, change yourself first.

要想改变命运,首先改变自己。

Progress is the activity of today and the assurance of tomorrow.

——Emerson

进步是今天的活动、明天的保证。

——爱默生

The ant is the most industrious animal, but it most be scanty of words.

——Franklin

没有任何动物比蚂蚁更勤奋,然而它却最沉默寡言。

——富兰克林

If you have great talents, industry will improve it; if you can be flat, industry will supply their deficiency.

如果你很有天赋,勤勉会使天赋更加完善;如果你的才能平平,勤勉会补足缺陷。

Genius is hard work, someone once said. If this is not entirely correct, at least it is to a great extent right.

天才就是勤奋,曾经有人这样说过。如果这话不完全正确,那至少在很大程度上是正确的。

People who exercise their brains stay young in spirit.

善于思考,心态不老。

What generally passes for "thought" among the majority of mankind is the time one takes out to rearrange one's prejudices.

—— Clare Boothe Luce

大多数人所谓的"思考",是花时间重新审视自己的偏见。

—— 克莱尔·布思·鲁斯

Permanent success cannot be achieved except by incessant intellectual labour, always inspired by the ideal.

——Sarah Bernhardt

除非不断地努力思考，不断被理想所激发，否则我们无法得到永恒的成功。

——莎拉·伯恩哈特

The real purpose of books is to trap the mind into doing its own thinking.

—— Christopher Morley

书的真正作用是诱使大脑独立思考。

——克里斯托弗·莫利

Readers are plentiful; thinkers are rare.

—— Harriet Martineau

阅读的人很多，思考的人却很少。

—— 海丽叶特·马蒂诺

把握人生

I am the master of my fate and the captain of my soul.

——Invictus

我主宰着自己的命运,掌管着自己的灵魂。

——英维克特斯

Fortune is a disguised person. No face is more cheating than this face.

命运是一个乔装打扮的人,没有比这张脸更会欺骗人的了。

Destiny is not a matter of chance, it is a matter of choice; it is not a thing to be waited for, it is a thing to be achieved.

命运不是机遇问题,而是选择问题,不是要等待的东西,而是要实现的东西。

It is most easily to see one's morality in the destitution of fortune.

厄运中最容易看出一个人的气节。

If you are too fortunate you will not know yourself; if you are too unfortunate, nobody will know you.

太幸运,就会不知道自己是谁; 太不幸,就会没人知道你是谁。

Throw a lucky man into the sea and he will climb up the shore with a fish in his mouth.

把幸运的人扔到海里，他也会嘴里衔住一条鱼上岸。

For some, destiny is their mother who gave them birth, but a stepmother for others.

命运对有些人是生母，而对另有一些人却是继母。

Gold loses its luster when the good fortune leaves, and black iron glitters when it comes.

好运去，黄金失色；好运来黑铁生光。

I should collar the neck of fortune, never to be crushed by fortune.

我要扼住命运的咽喉，绝不为命运所压倒。

If fortune gives me a sour lemon, let us try to make it into sweet lemon juice.

当命运递过酸柠檬，设法把它做成甜柠檬汁。

Wherever we roam about, fortune always leads us ahead.

无论到什么地方，命运总是在前面引路。

In gloomy days don't let the cruel fortune laugh up in its sleeve; now that it humiliated us, we should retaliate in composed manner.

在灰暗的日子里,不要让残酷的命运窃喜;命运既然来凌辱我们,我们就应该用处之泰然的态度加以报复。

Prosperity is not without many fears and disasters whereas adversity is not without comforts and hopes.

顺境中并非不掺杂各种担心与祸患,而逆境中也并非不存在欣慰与期望。

Lot likes to withdraw at certain moments so as to let you make sustained efforts to call it back.

运气喜欢在某些时刻撤退,目的是让你通过切实努力把它召回来。

Fortune is like the market, where many times, if you can stay a little, the price will fall.

运气就像市场,常常是你能等待一会儿,价格就会下降。

Take not comfort, but courage, from another's distress, and be sure, whatever your misery, that there are some whose lot you would not exchange with your own.

不要从别人的不幸中获得安慰，而是要获得勇气；切记，无论你怎样不幸，有些人的命运比你还糟。

Fate is a chain of endless causes and efforts which everything lives on. The development of the world also follows the principle and relation.

命运是一根无尽因果和努力的链条，万事万物皆源于此。世界本身的发展也遵循这一准则与因果关系。

When Goddess of Fate is eager to make fun, she would raise people from gully to an extremely high position.

命运女神想开玩笑时，会把人从沟里举到天上。

At the critical moment of deciding one's fate, after losing all hopes, he becomes sharp-eyed and clear-headed.

在决定命运的关键时刻，一个人失去一切希望之后会变得心明眼亮。

Since fate is arranged by opportunity, we should know: everyone, ordinary or great, should design life by himself, thus, ideal may become true at some future time.

既然命运由机遇安排,我们就应该明白:每个人,无论是凡人还是伟人,都要设计自己的生活,这样,理想也许会在未来某个时刻变成现实。

Fortune is arbiter of half our actions, but she still leaves the control of the other half to us.

命运对我们的行动只有一半主宰权,把另一半支配权留给我们。

Change is what keeps us fresh. Change is what keeps us young.

变化可以让我们感到清新。变化可以使我们保持年轻。

Work is a mysterious thing; many of us claim to hate it, but it takes a grip on us that is so fierce that it captures emotions and loyalties we never knew were there.

工作是一件神奇的东西。我们中的很多人口口声声说不喜欢它,但它却紧紧抓住我们,甚至让我们付出我们不曾意识到的感情和忠诚。

Everyone is an explorer. How could you possibly live your life looking at a door and not open it?

每个人都是探险家。你怎么可能一生都看着门而不去开它呢?

What you discover on your own is always more exciting than what someone else discovers for you—it's like the difference between romantic love and an arranged marriage.

你自己发现的东西总是比别人为你发现的东西更让你激动——就像浪漫爱情和被迫结婚之间的区别一样。

If I give you my idea and you give me yours, then we each have two ideas, and together we have four.

如果我把我的主意给你,你把你的主意给我,那么我们各自就有了两个主意,加起来我们就有了四个主意。

Doing the best at this moment puts you in the best place for the next moment.

此刻做得最好,下一刻你就处在最佳位置。

Forget about the misfortunes you've encountered, but don't forget the times your luck has turned.

忘掉你遭遇的不幸,但不要忘记你时来运转的时刻。

Memories are the key not to the past, but to the future.

记忆不是过去的钥匙,而是未来的钥匙。

Each of us is the accumulation of our memories.

每个人都是记忆的积累。

To err is human; to admit it, superman.

人都犯错误,认错是超人。

When we seek to discover the best in others, we somehow bring out the best in ourselves.

当我们想发现别人身上最好的东西时,在某种程度上将我们自己最好的东西也带了出来。

Only a fool tests the depth of the water with both feet.

只有傻瓜才会将两只脚放进水里试探水的深浅。

In the midst of great joy, don't promise anyone anything. In the midst of great anger, don't answer anyone's letter.

狂喜之中,不要向任何人许诺任何事情;暴怒之中,不要回任何人的信件。

If you risk nothing, then you risk everything.

你什么事都不冒险,那就是什么事都在冒险。

Feed your soul—meditate, walk by the sea, listen to music, visit art galleries and historic buildings. If you do, you'll feel more balanced.

沉思冥想、海边漫步、欣赏音乐、参观画廊、造访古屋,以此充实心灵,寻求心理平衡。

Life is fine and enjoyable, yet you must learn to enjoy your fine life.

人生是美好的,但要学会如何享受美好的生活。

Life is real, life is earnest.

——W. Longfellow

人生是真实而又严肃的。

——W·朗费罗

Life is compared to a voyage.

人生好比是一次航程。

Man can only be free through mastery of himself.

——S. E. Morison

只有通过掌握自己，才能使自己得到解放。

——S·E·莫里森

The good or ill of man lies within his own will.

——Epictetus

人善良或邪恶在他自己的掌控之中。

——爱比克泰德

We are all connected to the great circle of life, as beings who live in the midst of nature, and return to nature.

生命是个大循环,生于自然,回归自然。

Time is a circus, always packing up and moving away.

时间是一个马戏团,总是在打点行装,匆匆离去。

Time is like an enterprising manager, who is always bent on staging some new and surprising production, without knowing very well what it will be.

时间像一位有进取心的经理,总是一心筹划某种令人吃惊的新产品,却不太明白那将是什么产品。

Not keeping an appointment is an act of clear dishonesty. You may as well borrow a person's money as his time.

爽约显然是一种没有诚信的表现。占人时间无异于借人金钱。

The unrestrainedness in youth makes a bill of exchange when old, which should be paid with the addition of interest after about thirty years.

青年时的放浪是晚年要支付的汇票,大约 30 年后要连本带息偿还。

Time provides the scope for the development of one's ability and other accomplishment.

时间为一个人的能力和才艺准备好了发展的地盘。

Time tries all things.

时间检验一切。

It is not by the gray of the hair that one knows the age of the heart.

白发多少,并不能告诉你一个人心灵的年龄。

Time is the biggest tyrant. In the course of our aging, he imposes taxes on our health, limbs, endowments, strength and facial features.

时间是最大的暴君。在我们衰老的过程中,他对我们的健康、四肢、才能、力气和相貌全部征税。

Time is also a great notary even in the moral court.

即使在道德法庭上时间也是伟大的公证人。

Old age is like climbing a mountain. The higher you climb, the more tired and breathless you become. But your view will be much more extensive.

老年像爬山。你爬得越高,就会越疲倦气喘,但你的视野就会越宽广。

There is no fence or hedge around time that has gone. You can go back and have what you like if you remember it well enough.

过去的岁月没有围墙和篱笆。如果你把它珍藏在记忆中,便可回到从前并重新获得你所喜爱的东西。

Fools expect tomorrow; wise men use tonight.

愚者指望明天，智者利用今晚。

Cherish a minute of time, as if sowing a fine seed. When the ground is blanketed with green trees with rich fruits, you will find the old man of time doesn't treat you unfairly.

珍惜一寸光阴，犹如播下一粒良种。待到绿满大地、硕果累累时，你会感到时光老人没有亏待你。

Death is no more than passing from one room into another.

死亡不过是从一个房间进入另一个房间。

The future is something everyone reaches at the rate of sixty minutes an hour, whatever he does, whoever he is.

未来是这样一件东西，每个人都以每小时 60 分钟的速度朝它走去，无论他做什么，无论他是谁。

Guard your time jealously and don't give up each minute; seek knowledge greedily, and try to acquire every bit of it.

严守时间，分秒不弃；渴求知识，争取点滴。

Time is grain for farmers.

对农民,时间就是粮食。

Time is wealth for workers.

对工人,时间就是财富。

Time is life for doctors.

对医生,时间就是生命。

Time is victory for strategists.

对战略家,时间就是胜利。

At 20 years of age the will reigns; at 30 the wit; at 40 the judgment.

20 岁凭意志; 30 岁看机智; 40 岁重判断。

The golden age is before us, not behind us.

黄金时代是在我们面前,而不是在我们背后。

Time works great changes.

时间会产生巨变。

The only effect of time has been to sift out the bad products; for nothing in literature can long survive but what is really good.

时间唯一的作用就是淘汰次品,因为只有真正的佳作才能流芳百世。

Time makes heroes but dissolves celebrities.

时间造英雄,但使名人淡出。

Those that make the best use of their time have none to spare.

充分利用时间的人不会有余暇。

From the angle of time, man is like the golden spot of the bright sunshine that glitters and elapses quickly.

从时间角度看,人就像艳阳中的金色斑点,一闪即逝。

The heavier is the load, the deeper is the footprint.

担子越重,脚印越深。

A change of fortune hurts a wise man no more than a change of the moon.

运气变化和月亮盈缺一样不会伤害智者。

Justice is a machine that, when someone has given it a starting push, rolls on itself.

正义是一台机器,一旦有人推一下就会自己转下去。

Desire beautifies what is ugly.

欲望会美化丑陋的东西。

The only man who is really free is the one who can turn down an invitation to dinner without giving any excuse.

——J. Renard

唯一真正自由的人是不用找任何理由就能谢绝宴请的人。

——J·勒纳尔德

We often hear of people breaking down from overwork, but in nine cases out of ten they are really suffering from worry or anxiety.

——John Lubbock

我们常听说某人因工作过度而累垮身体,但是实际上十有八九是因饱受担忧或焦虑的折磨。

——约翰·卢伯克

Time is a versatile performer. It flies, marches on, heals all wounds, runs out and will tell.

——Franklin P. Jones

时间是个多才多艺的表演者。它展翅飞翔，阔步前进，治愈创伤，飞逝而去，揭示真相。

——富兰克林·P·琼斯

Don't be fooled by the calendar. There are only as many days in the year as you make use of. One man gets only a week's value out of a year while another man gets a full year's value out of a week.

——Charles Richards

不要让日历蒙骗了你。一年有多少天仅仅取决于你利用多少天。有的人一年只得到了一个星期的价值，而有的人一个星期就能得到一整年的价值。

——查尔斯·里查德

All time management begins with planning.

——Tom Greening

时间管理始于计划。

——汤姆·格利宁

Each moment in history is a fleeting time, precious and unique.

——Richard Nixon

历史上的分分秒秒都转眼即逝,十分宝贵,意义独特。

——理查德·尼克松

Time tames strongest grief.

——Walt Kelly

再大的悲伤也能被时间所淡化。

——沃尔特·凯利

Don't anticipate trouble, or worry about what may never happen. Keep in the sunlight.

不要预言麻烦,也不要杞人忧天。要永远生活在阳光中。

Life is a process of accumulation. And you may fall sometimes, but even if you fall, you should understand how to grasp some sand in your hand.

人生是一个积累的过程。你总会摔倒,即使摔倒,也要懂得抓一把沙子在手里。

Life is like a box of matches. Stop using is foolish, but misusing it is dangerous.

人生像一盒火柴，不用属愚蠢，滥用却危险。

The challenge of life is to overcome.

人生的挑战在于征服。

Life is a do–it–yourself project.

生活就是一个自己动手的工程。

On the dance floor, as in life, you're only as good as your partner.

人生就像舞厅，只有舞伴配合，才能跳得好。

Adversity is sometimes hard upon a man; but for one man who can stand prosperity, there are a hundred that will stand adversity.

遭遇不顺对于一个人来说是痛苦的事，但在顺境中能把握自己的人是百里挑一。

It's no use abusing fate.

向命运叫骂无济于事。

Adversity is the trial of principle. Without it, a man hardly knows whether he is honest or not.

逆境是对原则的考验。没有它，一个人难以知道自己是否诚实。

Fate and temperament are two words for one and the same concept.

命运和气质是同一概念的两种说法。

A man's home is his castle.

一个人的家就是他的城堡。

Good order is the foundation of all things.

——Burke

良好的秩序是一切的基础。

——伯克

Nothing is more precious than independence and freedom.

—— Ho Chi Minh

没有什么比独立自由更可宝贵的了。

——胡志明

I like the dreams of the future better than the history of the past.

——T. Jefferson

我缅怀过去的历史,而更喜欢梦想未来。

——T·杰弗逊

Money is round. It rolls away.

——S. Aleichen

圆圆钱币,滚走容易。

——S·阿雷钦

He that will not allow his friend to share the prize must not expect him to share the danger.

不肯让朋友共享果实的人,不要指望朋友与他共患难。

Behavior is a mirror in which every one shows his image.

——Goethe

行为是一面镜子,反映出每个人的形象。

——歌德

Evil news rides fast, while good news baits later.

——John Milton

坏事传千里，好事不出门。

——约翰·弥尔顿

As the wheel of fortune has lifted him up to the top, it will lower him down to the bottom if the wheel turns on.

当命运之轮已把他抬到顶点时，如果这个轮子继续运转，必然会把他降到最低点。

To those who override fortune, confidence is the master of fortune.

对于能掌控命运者来说，信心是命运的主宰。

Sloth, like rust, consumes faster than labor wears.

——Benjamin Franklin

懒惰像生锈一样，比劳动更能消耗体力。

—— 本杰明·富兰克林

Habit is habit, and not to be flung out of the window by any man, but coaxed downstairs a step a time.

——Mark Twain

习惯就是习惯，谁也不能将其扔出窗外，只能一步一步地引它下楼。

——马克·吐温

It is discouraging to think how many people are shocked by honesty and how few by deceit.

——Coward

令人沮丧的是,对诚实感到吃惊的人不在少数,而对欺骗感到吃惊的人却寥寥无几。

——科沃德

The greater a man is, the more distasteful is praise and flattery to him.

——John Burroughs

一个人越伟大,对表扬和奉承就越反感。

——约翰·巴勒斯

Desire creates desire and then feels pain.

——Michelangelo

欲望激起欲望,欲望之后是痛苦。

——米开朗琪罗

The greater the man, the more restrained his anger.

——Ovid

人越伟大,越能克制怒火。

——奥维德

A light heart lives long.

——William Shakespeare

豁达者长寿。

——威廉·莎士比亚

Give a man a fish and he will eat for a day. Teach a man to fish and he will eat for the rest of his life.

授人以鱼,使之果腹一日; 授人以渔,使之饱食终生。

We grow neither better nor worse as we grow old but more like ourselves.

——M. L. Becker

随着年龄的增长,我们变得既不更好,也不更坏,而是变得更像我们自己。

——M·L·贝克尔

Healthy body is a drawing room for soul, but the weak body is a prison.

健康的身体是灵魂的客厅,病弱的身体则是灵魂的监狱。

He who tells a lie is not sensible of how great a task he undertakes, for he must be forced to invent twenty more to maintain that one.

撒谎者往往意识不到他在执行多么艰巨的任务，为了维持一个谎言必须再编出 20 多个谎言。

All men whilst they are awake are in one common world; but each of them, when he is asleep, is in a world of his own.

所有人在醒着时都是置身于同一个世界，但睡着后，却都置身在自己的世界。

You can make your world so much larger simply by acknowledging everyone else's.

你可以通过承认别人的世界而让你的世界大得多。

Souvenirs are perishable; fortunately, memories are not.

纪念品会消失，幸运的是记忆不会。

A good friend is cheaper than therapy.

好朋友有益于健康，花钱还少。

Life is not easy for any of us; that's something you learn when you have a close friend, and begin to understand the problems in their lives as well as your own.

生活对任何人都不容易,这是有了密友才了解的事情,开始理解生活中的问题是共同的。

Money and friendship don't mix. Don't borrow money from your friends, and don't lend it either, unless you can be sure you won't fall out over it.

金钱与友谊不能混为一谈,不要向朋友借钱,也不要借给朋友钱,除非你确信不会为此失去朋友。

Business, you know, may bring money, but friendship hardly ever does.

—— Jane Austin

生意会带来钱财,但友谊很少如此。

——简 · 奥斯汀

In life's trials and tribulations, it is to our friends that we look for comfort and reassurance.

生活面临考验与苦难时,我们从朋友那里寻求慰藉与安慰。

Friendship is a soothing balm to the soul.

友谊是安慰心灵的良药。

The problem with friendships at work is that, often, the environment is extremely competitive.

同事之间友谊的问题在于工作环境常常充满竞争。

Friends are a great comfort in times of trouble; but they're also a great delight in times of joy.

逆境中朋友送来很大安慰，快乐中朋友锦上添花。

Best friends don't always need to be present; they can keep you company in your heart.

最好的朋友无须总在一起，而是在心里陪伴你。

Caring and sharing; that's what friendship's all about.

相互关心与分享便是友谊的真谛。

Sometimes, people expect too much of their friends. Remember nobody's perfect!

有时人们对朋友的期望值过高。记住人无完人。

A friend is the person who will help you with the dullest of chores, and make them seem fun.

朋友帮你干最沉闷的苦活儿并让这些看起来很有趣。

Friends of the right kind will help you far more than money or success ever will.

合适的朋友比钱财和成功给你更多的帮助。

A friendship with no trust is like a cell phone with no network coverage. All you can do is play games!

没有信任的友谊就像没有网络覆盖的手机,能做的只是玩玩游戏而已。

The world is so empty if one thinks only of mountains, rivers, and cities; but to know someone who thinks and feels with us, and who, though distant, is close to us in spirit, this makes the earth for us an inhabited garden.

光想着群山、河流和城市,世界也太空旷了。如果认识一个心心相印、心灵相通的远方朋友,地球就是我们居住的花园。

The only way you may correct the bad things in your past is to add better things to your future.

——Shiloh Morrison

纠正过去的错误的唯一办法就是未来做些好事。

——士罗·莫里森

As you get older, don't slow down. Speed up. There's less time left.

——Malcolm Forbes

年龄大了,不要放慢速度,而要加快速度,剩下的时间不多了。

——马尔克姆·福布斯

There are no little events in life, those we think of no consequence may be full of fate, and it is at our own risk if we neglect the acquaintances and opportunities that seem to be casually offered, and of small importance.

——Amelia Barr

生活里无小事。我们认为无关紧要的小事也许事关命运。如果我们忽视好像偶然而至、无关紧要的熟人和机会,就是在冒险。

——阿米莉亚·巴尔

Justice is like a train that's nearly always late.

正义就像几乎总是晚点的火车。

True friendship, like true love may take time to grow.

真正的友谊如同真爱,需要时间培育。

The world is like a mirror: frown at it and it frowns at you; smile, and it smiles too.

世界如镜子:你朝它皱眉它就朝你皱眉,你朝它微笑它也朝你微笑。

Slit gallops by the aid of rapids, but it can't succeed in escaping the destiny of sinking, even if it gets to the sea.

泥沙借激流的力量而奔腾,但是即使到了大海,也逃脱不了沉没的命运。

Misery is like dark clouds, which is a block of darkness from a far distance, but just gray near.

苦难犹如乌云,远望漆黑一片,而身临其下不过是灰色而已。

Fortune is a little womanish, who stands away farther when you court her more often.

运气有点儿像女人，你越向她求爱，她越远离你。

Don't let life pass you by. Live in the present, savoring each moment.

不要让生命从身边溜走，抓住当下，珍惜每时每刻。

The only way to keep your health is to eat what you don't want, drink what you don't like, and do what you'd rather not.

保持健康的唯一方法是吃不想吃的东西，喝不爱喝的东西，做不愿做的事。

Enthusiasm and energy are great gifts in a personality, and can take one a very long way in life.

热情与精力是重要天赋，而且能长久陪伴。

Some people dream of success; others work for it.

有人梦想成功，有人努力成功。

Those who don't feel pain seldom think that it is felt.

没有经历过痛苦的人很少能想到别人的痛苦。

Where there's life, there's hope.

有生命的地方就存在希望。

Make today the start of a wonderful new adventure.

今天开启精彩的新冒险吧。

Chiefly the mold of a man's fortune is in his own hands.

人的命运主要掌握在自己的手里。

I believe that genius is an infinite capacity for taking life by the scruff of the neck.

——Christopher Quill

我认为天才就是具备掌控命运的无限能力。

——克里斯托弗·奎尔

Teach yourself well; do not try to teach others.

把自己教好,不要试图教别人。

No matter where to go, what the weather, always bring your own sunshine.

无论去哪儿,什么天气,记得带上自己的阳光。

The lamp of life for enthusiasm is lit, the boat of life for hard work moves on.

生命之灯为热情而点燃,生命之舟因拼搏而前行。

Life is not waiting for the storm to pass, but learn to dance in the rain.

生活不是等着暴风雨过去,而是学会在风雨中跳舞。

When you're honest with yourself, no one in the world can deceive you.

你对自己诚实,世界上谁也骗不了你。

People have to focus, to have a foothold. The former is strategy, the latter is tactics.

人要有着眼点,又要有落脚点。前者是战略,后者是战术。

Success is actually very simple, when you cannot hold, hold on for another minute.

成功其实很简单,就是当你坚持不住的时候,再坚持一下。

A beautiful face is for others to see, and a wise mind is used for oneself.

漂亮的脸孔是给别人看的,而有智慧的头脑才是给自己利用的。

No matter how horrible the reality, you have to believe that this is the temporary darkness before the dawn.

不管现实有多可怕,你都要相信,这只是黎明前暂时的黑暗。

Winners can tell you where they are going, what they plan to do along the way and who will be sharing the adventure with them.

——Denis Waitley

胜利者会告诉你他们要去哪里,一路打算做什么,谁与他们一起冒险。

——丹尼斯·魏特里

To promote cooperation and teamwork, remember: people tend to resist that which is forced upon them, and people tend to support that which they help to create.

——Vince Pfaff

促进团队合作要记住：人们往往抵触强加于他们的事情，支持他们帮着做的事情。

——文斯·普法夫

Those who are lifting the world upward and onward are those who encourage more than criticize.

——Elizabeth Harrison

那些推动世界向前发展的人靠的是鼓励而不是批评。

——伊丽莎白·哈里生

The real winners in life are the people who look at every situation with an expectation that they can make it work or make it better.

——Barbara Pletcher

生活中真正的赢家面对任何情况都认为能处理好，能完善。

——芭芭拉·普雷彻

Life is not always fair, get used to it.

——Bill Gates

生活并不总是公平的；要去适应它。

—— 比尔·盖茨

Life lies not in living but in liking.

生活不在于活着,而在于热爱人生。

Each of us makes his own weather, determines the color of the skies in the emotional universe which he inhabits.

在我们居住的情感世界中,每个人都在形成自己的天气,决定着自己天空的颜色。

Lollygagging can turn this world around, transform the angry to serene, the frenzied to placid and the stubborn to mushy.

——Ann Allen

悠闲可以改变世界:化愤怒为平静,化狂热为冷静,化固执为随和。

——安·艾伦

The main dangers in this life are the people who want to change everything — or nothing.

——Lady Astor

当下生活中的主要危险皆来自那些想改变一切或想一切都不改变的人。

——阿斯特夫人

Growing old is not upsetting; being perceived as old is.

——Kenny Rogers

越来越老并不让人苦恼，让人苦恼的是别人觉得你越来越老。

——肯尼·罗杰斯

Never let what you cannot do interfere with what you can do.

不要让不能为之事干扰能为之事。

Choose your friends, and your pleasures in life, with care.

生活中慎交友，少贪玩。

Those who say little are thought to be wise; those who say much are seen to be fools.

人们认为寡言者智，话多者傻。

Reliance on others is necessary in life; but make sure you allow others to be reliant on you, too.

生活中信赖别人是必要的，但要确保别人也能信赖你。

Don't envy others; they may have more problems than you know about, and may be struggling just as much as you are.

不要嫉妒他人，他们也许比你的问题还多，也许像你一样在挣扎。

The only wisdom we can hope to acquire is the wisdom of humility: humility is endless.

我们希望能得到的唯一智慧是谦虚的智慧：谦虚无止境。

The applause of a single human being is of great consequence.

——Samuel Johnson

一个人的喝彩也具有重要的意义。

——塞缪尔·约翰逊

Above all else: go out with a sense of humor. It is needed armor. Joy in one's heart and some laughter on one's lips is a sign that the person down deep has a pretty good grasp of life.

——Hugh Sidey

最重要的是要有幽默感。幽默感是必要的盔甲。发自内心的快乐和欢声笑语显示对生活有很好的掌控力。

——休·西堤

A man's actions show his character.

行为可显出一个人的品性。

Slow help is no help.

慢帮忙就是不帮忙。

To believe with certainty we must begin with doubting.

为了确信,必须先怀疑。

Aspire to treat everyone you meet with respect, courtesy, and kindness.

希望对你遇到的每个人都表示尊重、礼貌和善意。

I never met a man so mean that I was not willing he should admire me.

——Edgar Watson Howe

任何人赞赏我,我都很愿意。

——艾德加·沃特森·豪

A hero is someone who understands the responsibility that comes with his freedom.

在自由的情况下,理解自己的责任就是英雄。

Sometimes the question are complicated and the answers simple.

有时问题复杂,答案简单。

You never know what is enough until you know what is more than enough.

——William Blake

知道何为多余你才知道何为满足。

——威廉·布莱克

One does what one is; one becomes what one does.

——Robert Musil

做什么人造就什么事,做什么事造就什么人。

——罗伯特·慕希尔

A merry heart goes all the way.

生性乐天,终身受用。

A man is never more truthful than when he acknowledges himself as a liar.

——Mark Twain

承认说谎是最诚实的人。

——马克·吐温

All the art of living lies in a fine mingling of letting go and holding on.

——Henry Ellis

生活的艺术不外乎抓放得当。

——亨利·艾莉斯

Important principles may and must be flexible.

——Abraham Lincoln

重要的原则可以是也必须是灵活的。

——亚伯拉罕·林肯

What we see depends mainly on what we look for.

——John Lubbock

我们所见主要是我们所想见。

——约翰·卢伯克

Money never starts an idea; it is the idea that starts the money.

金钱不会出主意,而主意会出金钱。

Simplicity is the ultimate sophistication.

——Leonardo da Vinci

简约是成熟的最高境界。

——列奥纳多·达·芬奇

To make a man happy, add not to his riches, but take away his desires.

让一个人幸福不是增加其财富,而是取走其欲望。

Economy is the poor man's mint, and extravagance the rich man's pitfall.

节约是穷人的造币厂,浪费是富翁的陷阱。

If we have not quiet in our minds, outward comfort will do no more for us than a golden slipper on a gouty foot.

——John Bunyan

黄金拖鞋无法舒缓痛风,外在享受无法安抚烦躁的心灵。

——约翰·班扬

A healthy, happy old age is a simple aim to aspire to, but very few of us achieve it.

健康幸福的晚年是个简单目标，人人渴求，但少有人达到。

The person who has health is young; the person who owes nothing is rich.

拥有健康便是年轻，没有外债便是富有。

Suffering is caused by craving. Stop craving, and your suffering will cease.

有所求会带来痛苦，放弃所求，痛苦便会随之消失。